FIGHTS YOU'LL HAVE AFTER HAVING A BABY

A Self-Help Story

MOLLIE PLAYER

Copyright (C) 2021 Mollie Player

Layout design and Copyright (C) 2021 by Next Chapter

Published 2021 by Next Chapter

Back cover texture by David M. Schrader, used under license from Shutterstock.com

Mass Market Paperback Edition

This book is a work of fiction. Names, characters, places, and incidents are the product of the author's imagination and have been used fictitiously. Any resemblance to actual events, locales, or persons, living or dead, is purely coincidental.

All rights reserved. No part of this book may be reproduced or transmitted in any form or by any means, electronic or mechanical, including photocopying, recording, or by any information storage and retrieval system, without the author's permission.

For free ebooks and online serials by Mollie Player, visit mollieplayer.com.

For Claus. Thank you.

This story is a fictionalized blend of several true stories.

1

The Beginning

Everyone told me it was normal to be nervous. More than nervous—freaked out. Insecure. *You're going to let us take her home now? By ourselves?* they remembered thinking before leaving the hospital. *Are you sure that's such a good idea?*

And actually, it was pretty weird. The nurses taught me how to latch the baby, how to change a diaper, how to adjust the straps on the car seat. They helped Matt and I get the swaddle neat and tight. But they didn't say a word about, well, parenting. Crib or bed? Feeding schedule or no? Go back to work or stay at home? All of the hard decisions were saved for another day, not this day, the day Poppy was born.

I labored at the hospital, Matthew there and gone again, making trips between the delivery room, various eating establishments and home. While he distracted himself with errands, I distracted myself with an audio book, trying not to wish he was nearby. Thing was, I didn't want him there. I really didn't. I didn't want to have to have a conversation. But if he would have held me—just that, and nothing more—that might have been all right.

It took two hours for the pitocin to kick in, and in

late afternoon the real labor came. For this, Matthew did hold me, both my head and my hand, offering his body as leverage. When the midwife told me to curl, Matthew pushed my legs to my head, and laughed at how hard I pushed back. Lots of pushes. Lots. So many. So many. Then the head was visible, and the midwife asked if I wanted a mirror.

"Yes!" I said.

"No," said Matt at the same time. Then: "You do, Hon? Are you sure?"

"Yes," I said. "Of course I do. Don't you?"

The midwife positioned it for me, and I saw my baby for the first time.

It didn't look like a baby.

Three more pushes. Hard pushes. Long ones. Then: relief. The head was out, and with a last push for the body, Matthew and I became parents.

Matthew looked at the baby, then at me. "It's a girl," he announced.

"We know that already," I said, laughing.

"She's beautiful," he said.

"But we knew that, too."

"Of course we did. She is perfect."

The midwife put Poppy, now crying heavily, on my chest. As I smooshed my breast against her mouth, Matthew put his hand on her soft hair.

"There she is."

"There she is. She is ours."

———

LATE THAT NIGHT. Matthew gone again. He didn't want to sleep on the pull-out. And as I soon learned, it was just as well. No, not just as well; it was better.

I got to spend the whole night with just her.

No sharing. No small talk. No deciding. No details. No normal life stuff. Just life. Just the room, the dark, except the street lamps below the half-drawn blinds, and a simple light behind the bed dimmed to almost nothing.

So this is motherhood, I thought as I stared at Poppy's face. This is who I am now. Strange that I'm not scared. Everyone says you'll be scared. But I feel good. I feel confident. It feels simple.

Here's this little alive thing, sort of like a plant, except that I am her air and sunlight, her photosynthesis. She needs me completely, and I accept the challenge. That is the way this thing works.

It's the most straightforward relationship I've ever had.

Honestly, that was it. That was my conclusion. I would be the giver, she'd be the taker—and I was fine with that. It was when I expected something, when I needed someone to behave a certain way—that was the situation I worried about.

Which is why lying in bed that night, there was only one thing I was worried about, and it had nothing to do with the baby.

It was Matthew.

What's he going to be like, now that we have a kid? I wondered. Will he be the same person? For that matter, will I? Will being parents affect the way we treat each other? How we are together?

How will our relationship change?

And as it turned out, I was right to be nervous. Because while that first year with Poppy was one of the best of my life, it was the worst for me and Matt.

———

THE FOLLOWING DAY, the hospital. Only that room in the hospital, and the bathroom adjoining it. Nothing more. Matthew came and went, bringing meals, bringing news. We opened a few presents, saw doctors, did paperwork. I slept a bit, too, Poppy next to me on the bed, though the nurse had advised against it. When I had to change my pad, the nurses helped me to the bathroom. They changed all of Poppy's diapers and held her when she cried. It was the first time in my life I'd been waited on so thoroughly, and I relished it. I didn't want to leave.

The following morning, Matthew arrived at 9 a.m. to take me home, and I delayed the departure as long as possible. When the time finally came—it was close to noon—I took a long last look at the room.

Maybe it was nostalgia. Sentimentality. Hormones. Or maybe—just maybe—it was more than that. Maybe it was the inkling I'd had the night before about Matthew.

Maybe I was sensing the learning curve ahead.

Yes, that was it. Just hours after giving birth, I had the mom thing figured out. I didn't know how to do anything—not even change a diaper—but I knew how to be alone with my child. But four years into my marriage, I still didn't know what Matthew expected of me, what he didn't expect of me, and, most important, what to expect of myself. When it was just Matthew and I, this oversight didn't matter. I compensated for not understanding what he really needed by giving him more of what he wanted, which worked fine. But now—now I had a second relationship to consider. My usual coping strategies wouldn't work.

Even before Matthew and I arrived home the tension between us had begun. Matthew wasn't himself. He was irritable. Hurried. Though whether due to jealousy, neglect or just impatience, I'll never know.

He tried to hide his annoyance with humor. "Should've had a home birth."

I responded with a tight smile and forced laugh. "I liked it there," I said.

"Yeah, I noticed. Thought you were going to sprain an ankle so you could stay."

"Don't begrudge me my reward," I told him, smiling again. "Besides, I thought about it. Wouldn't've worked."

The things I didn't say: "Why do I have to bring up the pain of childbirth this soon?" "Why aren't you happier?" "Why aren't we celebrating?" I wanted the day we left the hospital to be special, an occasion. Instead, I just felt sad to go home.

Maybe it was too much to expect him to know how I felt, how I wanted him to support me on that day. But a small gesture made in that tender time would've gone a long way towards lessening my fears. He could've held my hand. He could've told me how proud he was of me. He could've just asked me what I needed. It would've taken so little, almost nothing —but instead, he chose jokes and I chose smiles.

The first two weeks after the baby was born, I cried nearly every night before sleep. A few times, Matthew heard me; he came to the bedroom and asked what was wrong. Each time I told him the same thing.

"It's just hormones, Hon. I'll be okay."

I was working too hard. That was part of the problem. I always had and didn't want to stop. Baby in the chest carrier, I cooked, cleaned and, my favorite, organized. There's never an end of things to organize.

Part of me realized the emotions were normal, and that I wasn't taking good enough care of myself. Another part of me, though, blamed Matthew.

He wasn't helping enough. That's the truth, unvarnished. He didn't seem to know how to, really. While my life had changed completely—no more day job, constant sleep interruptions—he was quickly back to his usual routine. Work. Eat. Play. Sleep. Weekends: basketball, projects. Which is why, during those first few weeks with Poppy, I felt all the good stuff you're supposed to feel— gratitude and love—I felt a lot of bad stuff, too. I was scared. I was angry. But mostly, I was sad. Sad that things weren't right with me and Matt.

2

Change Your Story

Afterwards, I called it the Muffin Incident. Because though it wasn't exactly a fight, it was significant enough to name. It happened in December when Poppy had just reached three weeks of age and Matthew's mom, Mary, was visiting.

I'd taken a walk with Poppy, who had by now established herself as a fairly high-maintenance child. The stroller calmed her and the walking calmed me, and even in the coldest weather I didn't go a day without at least one long outing.

When I returned home, I was tired and thirsty and I badly needed to pee. I opened the door to see Mary sipping tea and Matthew on the couch, his bathrobe still on, even though it was eleven in the morning.

"Hello," I said.

Mary stood. "Nice walk?"

"It was."

Mary turned to her son. "Now, this is when you step in, Matthew, and take the baby so Rachel can get her shoes off and settle in."

I smiled tensely. Matthew did as he was told. Then I escaped to the kitchen. I got a glass of water and was heading to the bathroom when it happened: Matthew asked the question.

"Can you make me a muffin, honey?"

I paused, took it in. Emotion rushed to my head. My throat started to close, but I caught it, swallowing.

"Sure," I told him. "Just a minute."

I went to the bathroom, then to the kitchen, made him the muffin and brought it to the table. He sat down to eat, handing the baby back to me, and I sat on the couch and nursed.

As we chatted with Mary, I reflected on the exchange, not objectively, but honestly nonetheless. Mary wasn't just telling Matthew to take the baby at the front door, I mused. She was telling him to be more thoughtful. She was telling him to take the baby when I brush my teeth, do the laundry— whenever he's available and I'm not.

She was telling him to be more involved.

And yet, here I am—exhausted, overworked— holding the baby so my husband can eat a muffin. Why doesn't he get it? What am I doing wrong? I should've said something. But what?

Don't get me wrong: I didn't regret my choice not to argue. Mary was there, for one, but it was more than that. Thing is, Matt and I never fought. We prided ourselves on our self-control, our marital harmony. Now here we were, new parents, and the last thing I wanted was for that stability to be compromised.

It was too soon. I was too tender. I was only three weeks postpartum. Our first fight after having a baby would happen eventually. I just didn't want it to happen right then.

Evening came. By then, I'd replayed the incident two dozen times. In later versions the I-should'vesaids were expertly phrased and placed at the perfect, most humbling moment.

Matthew asks me for a muffin. A one-second pause. Then I reply, without breaking my gaze.

"I'm thirsty, I'm exhausted, and I badly need to pee, and you're still wearing your pajamas and talking to your mom. How long have you been sitting there, waiting for me to get home so you could eat? Or do you not even get hungry when I'm not there?"

By bedtime, I'd branched out. My thoughts grew and sprouted thick foliage, reaching into every aspect of our relationship. I questioned the basis of our marriage, Matthew's ability to be a good father. But mostly, I questioned his character.

Is Matthew a good person? I wondered, starting at Poppy. Or have I been deceiving myself somehow? Maybe when I fell in love, I ignored all the signs? Maybe Matt isn't who I thought he was.

Yeah. Those kinds of thoughts. They were ruthless.

The feelings I had that night reminded me of the day in high school when my best friend moved away; they were that pitiful. However, there was one consolation.

Though on that night and those to follow I was convinced my fears would still be there in the morning, every morning when I looked for them, they were gone.

STILL, about three weeks into parenthood, it finally dawned on me: This problem wasn't one to wait out. It wasn't going to go away. It wasn't going to fix itself. I'd have to find a way to get rid of it. So, I did what any other self-respecting self-help junkie would do: I started collecting advice.

I searched the Internet, of course, as well as the library. This was a lot harder than it sounds. Most of the relationship advice online was generic, to say the least. And the books I found didn't seem to address parenting. *What I need,* I decided, *is real stories, real experiences. I need to call a few friends.*

My first choice: calm, collected mother of four, Marianne.

Marianne was one of the happiest people I knew, and for good reason: She had the whole Zen thing figured out. While my habit was to analyze a problem from every angle, suffocating it with my prolonged attention, Mare knew how to just finesse things away. She knew how to let things be until they weren't—until they either died of boredom or left.

"Is this normal?" I asked after briefly explaining the situation. "Is this just the way new dads are?" What I really wanted to ask, though, was more personal, more probing: What had Marianne's own husband been like when their kids were born? But I didn't dare.

"I don't know if it's normal," Marianne replied. "But is that really the question you should be asking? Or should you just ask if it's something you can live with? If you're okay with what he's doing, or if you're not?"

Sensible advice, I thought, taking a deep breath. *Balanced, like Marianne herself.*

Maybe I asked the wrong person.

"Yeah, sure, I get it," I said. "There are no right answers, and all that. But what would you do if you were me? If you had this situation to deal with?"

"I know you want advice. All I can say is, think it over. Take a long walk. Pray about it a little. I know you're not religious, but try it, anyway. Then get really quiet and ask yourself what the answer is."

"That's all you got?"

Change Your Story

"That's it."

"Okay."

"Okay. And let me know what happens."

Yeah, I thought as I hung up the phone. *I definitely asked the wrong person. I don't need philosophy. What I need is help. I know. I'll call Gen instead.*

"I need to fix this," I whispered to Genevieve later that evening after I'd moved out of the office and away from Matthew. "I'm hormonal, and I'm miserable, when I should be the happiest I've ever been. This sucks. There must be something I can do."

"I know. There should be. There's got to be," said Gen. "It's almost impossible that nothing you can do will make a difference."

"Exactly," I said. "You get it. My fellow control freak. So, let's come up with some ideas."

"Have you read any marriage books yet?"

"Of course I have."

"Of course you have. So? What did they say?"

"Meh. The usual stuff. They were pretty bland. Nothing I haven't heard before."

"Maybe you read the wrong ones. Or maybe you need to branch out a bit. You know what I would do? I'd look for relationship advice in other kinds of books."

"Like what?"

"Like spiritual books. And parenting books. And psychology books—happiness research, that kind of thing."

"Woah. Hold on there. You lost me at parenting books. I'm not going to have time for all that reading."

"So skim it. Do what you can. I'll give you my notes, too. You can keep a journal of everything you learn that might help. What I've noticed is that when it comes to self-improvement stuff, if I don't write it down somewhere and keep a checklist, I forget it."

"Hmm. All right. That does make sense. If nothing else, it'll make me feel like I'm doing something."

"No, it'll work, Rachel. The answers are out there somewhere. You're not the first person to have these problems."

"No, I'm not. But that doesn't mean they're solvable."

"Rachel. Snap out of it. Matthew is great. He's not perfect, but he's ... basically normal. It's hard to see it when you're mad, but trust me. He's fixable. If anybody is fixable, he is."

"So what you're saying is I should try to change my partner? Isn't that supposed to be the worst relationship advice ever?"

"They only bad advice is the advice that doesn't work. And if you never try, you'll never know."

"That is true."

I hung up. I put Poppy in her swing, then, while making dinner, considered both my friends' advice.

I love Gen's practicality, I thought. *But Marianne's advice is easier. I think a long walk is in order.*

After a short dinner, I told Matt I'd be back in an hour. I put Poppy in the stroller and headed to a well-lit park. As I walked, I spoke out loud about my feelings, about my anger, about each and every perceived relationship problem. Then, I did as Marianne instructed: I got very quiet, and imagined my higher self giving me advice. It took just a few minutes for a small miracle to occur.

For the first time, I clearly heard my inner voice.

It was just a sentence—just a handful of words—and I heard it only in my thoughts, silently. But it came with a knowing, with a rightness, with a force.

And the words were definitely not my own. They were: "Change your story about Matthew."

What the hell was that? That was my first reaction. *It was followed by, Where did it come from?*

Was it an angel? Or did I make it up myself? Naw. That's the last thing I'd come up with. Denial? Can't be good. Especially about my marriage.

My subconscious is smarter than that.

I took a deep breath. Then another, and another. "It's time to head back," I said to Poppy.

Then, on the way home, something strange happened. The sentence I heard changed shape in my mind. I found myself remembering the early days of my relationship with Matthew, when things were so simple, so easy. Rare were the times when I questioned Matthew's character or motives, even when I disagreed with his choice. When he didn't bring me flowers on my birthday, for instance, he just wasn't into romantic displays. When he lost his temper over a tricky repair job, he was just tired or hungry.

Change your story about Matthew, I repeated to myself. *Yeah, there is some truth there. Matthew isn't without flaws. But he's who he is. He's doing the best he can.*

Like all of us, he's learning. He's trying. And when I remember that, our disagreements don't feel quite so horrible.

When I got home, I gave Matthew the baby and started getting ready for bed. As I did, I noticed something: I felt better. Lighter. Less angry, more hopeful that things would work out.

So this is what all those religious people feel, I thought, adjusting my blankets.

I felt a little transformed.

"Change your story." It just might work. But can I actually do it?

BEFORE POPPY WAS BORN, the answer would've been an easy yes. Back then, it was just so … straightforward. Maybe that's why the challenges Matthew and I experienced during our first several years of parenthood were so difficult for us to face.

They were just so unexpected.

Part of the reason for this was our relative maturity: We met at twenty-six, had kids at thirty. Plus, we weren't angry by nature; in the old lovers-versus-fighters split, neither of us could claim any affiliation with the latter.

If anything, in the first four years of our relationship, we didn't disagree enough. Before Poppy was born, chore distribution wasn't a problem. Matthew worked full-time and I worked part-time and cleaned and cooked. Meals were always on time and sleep was logistically uncomplicated, and our spending habits and social habits were compatible. Which is why, as we entered parenthood, our conflict resolution skills were notably underdeveloped.

Before Poppy, our relationship hadn't been tested.

Not to say, of course, that our pairing was seamless; we did have a few key personality differences. Matthew was lighthearted while I was serious and driven. He preferred to just get things done, while I was more of a dot-and-crosser. Matthew procrastinated, too, which drove me crazy, and he was easily annoyed by little stuff like traffic. I usually kept my head over the small stuff, but let the big stuff get to me, which I admit was no healthier.

But Matthew was nice. He held me when I cried, and respected my decisions, and listened. Almost half a decade into our relationship, we still chatted late into the night. We still truly liked each other. We were still best friends.

We were among the lucky ones—and we knew it.

Which is why one night during my pregnancy we had a conversation that went something like this:

"You know, they say having kids changes your relationship—that you start fighting more, getting angry," I said. "What do you think? Will that happen to us?"

We were lying in bed, Matthew on his back and me on my side facing him. The light was off, and in order to see Matthew's face better, I readjusted my pillow.

"I don't think it will," Matthew said, staring at the ceiling.

"Really, Hon? That's a nice thing to say."

Matthew turned to face me. "Well, what would we fight about?"

"I'm not sure," I said. "What is something that bothers you about me? They say that whatever it is, it'll get worse."

"Nothing comes to mind."

"Really? You can't think of even one thing?"

"Not really. Nothing important. Why? Can you?"

I pulled my arm off Matthew's stomach and rolled onto my back. "No," I said. "I can't, either. But I do kinda wonder if we'll remember this conversation later and laugh about how optimistic we were."

"Maybe," he said. And then he laughed.

Then our conversation shifted to more immediate concerns.

The feeling of invincibility we shared was, of course, overconfident—maybe even just plain dumb. However, in the years to come, whenever I recalled that moment, I realized it was also pretty sweet.

We believed in ourselves, and in each other, that much.

Even belief, though, arguably the most powerful

force in the Universe next to love and gravity, has its limitations.

It wasn't enough to keep us from fighting.

THE DAY after my decision to change my story about Matthew, nothing particularly notable occurred. And yet, there was a change: subtle, yet obvious. I sensed that Matthew sensed my new perspective. Maybe it was my eyes—softer now, easier. Maybe it was my tone of voice, my body movements. Whatever it was, the small differences truly made a difference, even though for a long time that's all there were.

Matthew was more helpful. He was happier. He bought me flowers. But the best changes were the less obvious ones. There were more smiles, more loving conversations—and a lot more conversations overall. It was like since Poppy was born we'd been living in a bubble of irritation without knowing it and suddenly the bubble popped and disappeared. Together we realized what we'd been missing out on.

We realized we were breathing again.

OF COURSE, seeing the best in my husband wasn't all it took to overcome the assault of early parenthood; for me, doing so took three years of fighting and learning. Which is why during those three years, my advice-collecting practice continued in earnest till my list of lessons looked something like this:

- Change Your Story
- Don't Fight; Just Talk Instead
- Don't Make It Into a Big Deal
- Be Uncomfortably Nice

- Shamelessly Bargain
- Apologize Every Chance You Get
- Brush Up on Your Endocrinology
- Change Your Partner the Right Way
- Don't Defend Yourself
- Appreciate the Gift

Admittedly, some of the advice was odd. Simplistic. Optimistic. Overly so, probably, on all counts. But when I followed it, a funny thing happened: my perspective on my relationship changed dramatically. No longer did I feel overwhelmed by the task before me, that of ensuring my marriage survived parenthood intact. The tricks gave me confidence in my husband, in my relationship skills and, finally, in myself.

They make me feel like I had some power.

There was only one problem: At times, I was unable to use that power. When I first set out on my parenting adventure, I realized it wouldn't be easy. What I didn't predict was the magnitude of my emotions, their ability to override all logic. Because of this, and because of the challenges Matthew and I faced, things did change in my marriage after we became parents, just as I feared they would.

And some of those changes were permanent.

My Relationship Journal: December
Lesson: Change Your Story

BOOK NOTES AND QUOTES:

DAN SAVAGE in an interview on StarTalkRadio.net:

- "What I'm constantly noticing is people … can be very articulate and long-winded about their partner's faults … and nowhere near as long-winded or articulate about their partner's strengths or what's good about their relationship."

SHAUNTE FELDHAHN in *The Surprising Secrets of Highly Happy Marriages:*

- Your partner's behaviors and reactions are often triggered by your approach. When you keep your cool in tense situations, they likely will, too.
- "By expecting the best, you bring out the best."
- "Highly happy couples always assume good intentions."

AARON BECK (one of the founders of CBT) in *Love Is Never Enough: How Couples Can Overcome Misunderstanding:*

- Whereas new couples are often positively biased toward each other, long-term couples are often negatively biased. This causes them to misinterpret each other's motives and intentions—and during emotional arguments, these misinterpretations tend to multiply.
- Cognitive Behavioral Therapy (CBT) is the most proven method for shifting this bias and other stories you tell yourself about your partner. It involves recognizing your assumptions and negative beliefs, questioning and testing

them, and reframing your perspective on the issue.

DAVID BURNS in the best-selling CBT book *The Feeling Good Handbook*:

- When we question and dispute our negative beliefs, our accompanying negative feelings become less persistent and less convincing.
- Whenever you're experiencing an especially negative emotion, journal about it. Write down the reasons your stressful thought might be either exaggerated or entirely untrue, and reframe the situation in a more positive, objective light.
- "If you want to feel better, you must realize that your thoughts and attitudes—not external events—create your feelings."

WILLIAM BACKUS AND MARIE CHAPIAN in *Telling Yourself the Truth: Find Your Way Out of Depression, Anxiety, Fear, Anger, and Other Common Problems by Applying the Principles of Misbelief Therapy*:

- Always remember that there are at least two versions of the truth. Then consistently choose to believe the more agreeable one. People who struggle a great deal with anger or depression often choose the version with fewer truth elements than people who are more optimistic.
- Often, but not always, relationships

change dramatically when one person drops the misbeliefs that generate and perpetuate bitterness and anger. Always the person who works to change misbeliefs will benefit even if the other person does not change.

PROVERBS 10:12 in *The Holy Bible:*

- "Hatred stirreth up strifes: but love covereth all sins."

MY RELATIONSHIP RESOLUTIONS:

- I will remind myself that Matthew's motives are good. I won't automatically infer uncaring feelings, as is often my knee-jerk response when upset. Instead, I'll either assume the intentions behind his words and actions are good, or I'll simply ask him to explain them.
- I will remind myself that Matthew's character is good. I won't start a monologue in my mind listing all of his past similar actions, and drawing conclusions about how he will act in the future. Instead, I'll make giving him the benefit of the doubt a habit.
- I won't hear insults where insults aren't spoken. Instead, I will hear need. I'll hear tiredness, stress, sadness, hunger—or maybe just a desire to feel loved.
- I won't play judge or jury. No matter what my partner does, whether "good" or "bad," desirable or not, there's no reason for me to judge his character. If a behavior doesn't work for me, it doesn't

work for me; I can recognize that, communicate it to him without anger. The thoughts that drive me crazy are the ones that aren't needed, thoughts like: "Is he a good husband?" "Is he a good person?" "How's his character?" In the end, all these questions are nonsensical. In some moments, my partner is awesome—kind and surprisingly self-aware. In other moments, he has his blinders on. Any belief I have in my mind about your partner's character is ultimately just that: a belief. Nothing more substantial than that.

- I will practice CBT regularly.
- I will question any painful beliefs that come up about my partner and our relationship.

FOR THE FRIDGE:

- "I promise to believe your intentions are good."
- "I promise to double-check my story."

3

Don't Fight. Just Talk Instead

Two months into motherhood, I still hadn't gotten the hang of co-parenting. Though my hormones had largely normalized and the night crying had stopped, the tension between Matthew and I was still there. It came in waves—small ones, mostly, with the occasional whitecap. Though I did my best to withstand them one by one, it wasn't enough; I wanted to swim.

And then, the argument I'd been waiting for—that Matthew and I both, probably, knew was coming—finally happened.

It started, predictably, in the evening, when we were most tired and vulnerable. Despite the recent improvement in our feelings toward each other and in our overall communication, our core post-baby issues hadn't been addressed yet.

We still had some stuff to figure out.

Little by little, the frustration returned. Then the mouse took his place at the end of the rope, and pulled, and pulled again, and I came down with the flu.

It wasn't the worst flu I'd ever had. But it was one of the most unpleasant, if only because I couldn't lie in bed. I had to hold. I had to walk. I had to hit the damn button on the damn musical toy, staving off moment by moment a crisis of boredom from a child that couldn't yet work her own hands.

I had to mother a newborn while sick.

When I stopped any of these things, the crying started up again. And of course, it wasn't just crying. It was that wailing, tragedy-has-already-struck-and-I-don't-want-anyone-to-forget-to-save-me cry that serves our little humans so well.

Since it was a Saturday, Matthew was home all day, but unfortunately he wasn't much help. "Every time I pick her up, she just cries louder," he'd complain after what seemed like mere minutes of carrying. "She's probably hungry. She needs to nurse."

Then he'd hand Poppy back, and sit back on the couch.

Uncomfortable minutes became painful hours, and hours became a morning and an afternoon. Finally, sometime after the sun went down, I decided I couldn't take it anymore.

I decided I'd have to start a fight.

I couldn't just go to the bedroom without Poppy, leaving her with Matthew for a while. I couldn't calmly draw a bath and lock the door behind me. I couldn't gently ask Matthew to take Poppy out or, God forbid, simply talk to him about my feelings. All those choices were the choices of emotionally stable people, people with full reserves of self-control.

And right then, I wasn't one of them.

So, I did the only thing left for me to do. I stormed into the TV room, threw a toy on the floor, and, for the first time, screamed at him.

"Get off the couch! Help me with the baby! Get in here and play with Poppy!"

Matthew looked at me with surprised eyes, then with cold ones. Then he looked away without responding.

"Get up! Get up!" I said again, walking in front of him. "Get over here and take the baby right now!"

Matthew set his jaw tighter, still saying nothing. Seeing this, I crossed another line I hadn't crossed with him before: I swore.

"You are an asshole!" I yelled. "You are an asshole! There, I said it! Finally! I am sick, and overworked, and you're just watching TV, acting like it's not your problem!

"I am mad at you! I am mad at you! I am mad at you!"

The screaming was new. The cursing was new. But the most significant part of the outburst was the end. It was the first time I'd ever told Matthew, outright, that I was mad at him.

It was the first time I admitted there was a problem in our relationship.

Matthew stood up. He went to the playroom in silence and sat with the baby on the floor. I stormed off to the bedroom, slamming the door as loudly as possible. Then I lay in bed, feeling even more miserable than before.

Clearly, this fight isn't over, I knew. *But how best to talk it out? Should I wait till tomorrow when I'm feeling less emotional? Or should I go talk to him right now?*

I tried to read but couldn't focus on the book. Then I made a cup of tea I didn't drink. Finally, I realized I didn't want to spend the rest of the night avoiding the problem, distracting myself; what I really wanted to do was to talk.

I went to the playroom and sat on the floor against the wall a comfortable distance from Matthew and Poppy. When after a long moment Matthew finally looked at me accusingly I looked back sadly and started to cry.

"Honey, what's going on?" Matthew asked, hurt. I was relieved to hear his voice.

"I know, Hon, I know. I snapped. I shouldn't've said what I said. But really, I am so beyond my limit."

Matthew sighed.

"I know I've told you this before. But I don't think you really understand: I am so far, far beyond my limit. I'm exhausted. I'm working and sleeping and nothing else. And sometimes you don't even try to help."

"What are you talking about?" Matthew asked, bouncing Poppy in his lap. "I help almost every time you ask. Don't you notice?"

I paused. *He does?* "You do?"

"Absolutely."

"Wow. Wait a second while I rearrange my entire mental recording of our past few months."

"Yeah, do that."

"You think you help me a lot? And how often is a lot to you?"

"Often. A few times a day."

I took a deep breath. *Not only doesn't he help me enough—he doesn't even realize it,* I thought. *He really doesn't have a clue.*

"And what do you consider helping?" Another breath. Then another.

"The diapers and the cooking and the grocery shopping and playing with the baby when you need me to? You don't think I help? Wow. I feel so unappreciated."

"You feel … unappreciated?" I said. "You feel … unappreciated." And from that moment on, though we talked for several hours, nothing else of substance was said. The conversation that followed was frustratingly circular, and the resolution we came to far from adequate.

I pointed out what I felt was patently obvious: the number of hours I spent with the baby each day, the lack of significant breaks. Matthew defended his position—didn't give an inch—which, to me, was more than wrongheaded. It was betrayal.

"And here this whole time I've been so proud of myself, sacrificing so much for our daughter. I've missed so much sleep. I've done almost everything for her. And you think changing a few diapers actually compares? I have never felt more unloved in my life."

Matthew pointed out that though I was with Poppy during the day, he couldn't be; he was at work. "Anyway, we talked about this. We decided I'd take the baby every night while you make dinner. And that is exactly what I've been doing."

"Don't you get it, Matthew? Don't you see what I'm going through? When you take the baby in the evening, I'm still working; I'm getting dinner. Then you go off and have your time alone, but when do I ever get a break?"

"You never ask for a break."

"I never ask for a break? Isn't it obvious that when your wife is sick, she could use a little help? Isn't that just human decency and compassion? Besides, when I do ask, you get moody about it, and I feel like even though you say you'll help, you don't want to. Sometimes it's just easier not to ask."

"Well, you've been pretty moody lately, too, you know. It's not fun for me, either."

I shook my head. "Wow. So an hour a day of help is enough in your mind. You really have no idea."

"If you need more help, Hon, you need to ask for it."

"Fine. I will. Remember this conversation when I do, though, and you say no or get annoyed."

"Fine with me." A long pause. "I'm tired. I'm going to bed."

That night as we lay next to each other, not touching, I surprised myself; I decided to move my legs over and rub them against Matthew's. Because, in spite of everything, in spite of my anger and my disappointment, I was glad that he was there.

"I'm going to try to communicate better with you," I told him in the dark.

"And I will help you more with Poppy," he replied.

Then we both said "I love you," and went to sleep.

———

IN THE WEEKS following our first big fight after having a baby—the Post-Baby Brawl we'd been waiting for—my fearful nighttime thoughts were more frequent and disastrous than ever. First, I returned to the previous theme of questioning Matthew's character: *Matthew is a selfish person, a taker, inconsiderate in the extreme.* But I found even those thoughts could be topped.

My whole life is a sham. I go around pretending that everything is okay, but it's not; a lot of days, I'm barely hanging on. I'm never going to solve my relationship problems. It's impossible. He will never change.

One afternoon about a month after the argument, I put Poppy in the carrier and took her to the nearest running track for an easy, undistracted walk. I didn't want to think about the scenery or where to turn next; I just wanted to focus on my thoughts. When we arrived, the park was empty, and I decided to take the opportunity to speak my feelings out loud, try to untangle them.

"How does everyone do it?" I asked myself. "There's got to be something I'm missing. My friends, people I know—they have kids and recommend it. They seem happy with their partners despite the challenges. What do they know that I haven't figured out yet? Is there something here I need to learn?

"I just feel so lost. I don't know what to do, how to get through to him. It's obvious to me that he needs to do more. But there are only so many different ways I can ask him. I'm angry so often, and I hate it."

Then a thought came. A feeling, really, much like the one that came a month prior. Like its predecessor, it came with a rightness, with a force of knowing —and even with a bit of peace.

"What if you tried not showing Matthew your anger?" it said. "What if you just had a lighthearted conversation? There is no rule that says you have to be honest all the time about your feelings. You can fake it a little—smile, make a joke. Even when you're mad, you don't have to fight. You can say nothing, or just talk."

I rounded the next curve in silence, letting the thought sink in. I didn't quite know what to make of it. Hadn't I always heard that it's good for couples to fight, to vent their feelings before they grew into resentment? If I never yelled at Matthew, how would he know that he hurt me? What would motivate him to do better?

Soon, good sense set in. *Of course*, I thought. *A smile. A joke. Learning how to just talk. I can show Matthew how I feel without yelling.*

I can be mad, but not fight

Wow.

For the rest of the walk, I contemplated the advice further, and by the time I reached home, I had a plan. In addition to always assuming the best of Matthew, I would attempt to never show him my anger—to only either speak nicely or be silent.

Though the months that followed proved the plan difficult, even impossible, to carry out flawlessly,

I never stopped believing in its effectiveness—and the more I practiced it, the easier it became. Far from adding to my resentment, it helped me keep my perspective.

Just talking, it turned out, was pretty awesome.

Why didn't anyone teach me this sooner? I wondered. *I guess there's a point to marriage after all.*

My Relationship Journal: March
Lesson: Don't Fight. Just Talk Instead.

BOOK NOTES AND QUOTES:

SHAUNTE FELDHAHN in *The Surprising Secrets of Highly Happy Marriages:*

- Forget the old advice and *do* go to bed angry. It's best to talk over a problem when you're detached and level-headed.

DANIEL SIEGEL in *Mindsight: The New Science of Personal Transformation:*

- Our brains are hard-wired for conflict and danger. Due to our heritage of difficult survival conditions, we're often on the lookout for anything that threatens our sense of well-being—even in our relationships.
- When people get mad, the anger part of the brain (the amygdala) becomes highly active. This activity then partially overrides or obscures the activity in the places of the brain that are responsible for logic and reason. "I wasn't acting like

myself," then, isn't just a lame excuse for bad behavior. There is a lot of truth to it. Therefore, it's best to wait out the anger before discussing a problem with your spouse.

TARA PARKER-POPE in *For Better: How the Surprising Science of Happy Couples Can Help Your Marriage Succeed:*

- The most important part of an argument is the first few minutes, when the tone is (sometimes irreversibly) set. Carefully plan the way you'll bring up a tender topic with your partner.
- It is far better to start an argument with a complaint—a simple explanation of a struggle—rather than with a criticism, which quickly gets personal and derails the conversation.
- While arguing, speak slowly and quietly. This is huge.
- Also, use key phrases that help de-escalate an argument, such as: "It sounds like you're saying," "It seems like," "What if," "I know this is hard for you," "What are your thoughts?" and many more.

CANDACE PERT in *Everything You Need to Know to Feel Go(o)d:*

- Emotions are real. They're physical, molecular entities that exist inside your brain.
- Each emotion is made up of cell receptors and the signals that direct them, plus ligands–protein precursors. Each

receptor wiggles and sends vibrations to attract the proper ligand, like a lock and key mating. These vibrations and their constant responses form a continuous electrical current throughout your body that we feel as emotion.
- Once a feeling is well-established, it doesn't die (give up its place in your body) without an attempt to resist. When cell receptors don't find the right ligands, the hypothalamus signals thoughts in the brain that attract the right ligands to it. This happens even with negative emotions, like anger.
- To rewire your brain to get angry less often, regularly visualize a different outcome, idea or emotion. Eventually, the cell receptors and ligands will get tired of failing, and get pruned.

MY RELATIONSHIP RESOLUTIONS:

- I will perform a pre-fight cost benefit analysis. Is the best possible outcome worth having the argument?
- I will start no unnecessary fights. Simple as that. When I get mad at Matthew about something minor, I'll just let it go. The resentment won't kill me; to the contrary, it'll die out more quickly.
- If I decide the fight is worth it, I will wait a while before bringing it up.
- Rather than fighting, I will learn how to just talk. No snapping. No sarcasm. No condescension. No crankiness, even. I might even find space for a joke.
- I will focus on solutions.

- I will use "I" statements.
- I will not expect a verbal apology. I will understand that sometimes, apologies are disguised as actions rather than words.
- Above all, I will use a kind, respectful tone of voice.

FOR THE FRIDGE:

- "I promise not to discuss an issue unless it's worth the tension it will cause and unless I've given it some time."

4

Don't Make It Into a Big Deal

With that first big fight after having our baby an invisible barrier was breached. Gradually, over the course of our first half-year of parenthood, our arguments became not exactly frequent, but much less unexpected than before. Granted, they were quiet fights, usually—no yelling, no slamming doors.

But they were definitely still fights.

On the surface, the topics were few—sort of a greatest hits situation: Matthew's long hours at work, my long days at home, undone chores. But now we had an even bigger problem: even when we weren't actually arguing, there was an atmosphere of impatience.

In other words: we were moody.

Day by day, small annoyances were piling up, much like the dishes in our increasingly neglected kitchen sink. Misplaced belongings. Forgotten diaper bags. Car trouble. All the things that get under our skin even when we aren't already on edge were accumulating, taking on greater significance for their number. Matthew's bad attitudes caused my bad attitudes and vice versa, until we both felt we were the one being wronged the most. As a new, often overwhelmed mom I desperately wanted Matthew to be the strong one, to put a smile on his face and "take one for the team." But that isn't how relationships work, is it? I had to be the better one, the more enlightened one, the more mature one. Me. If I wanted anyone to. Only me.

And so, as month five approached, the tension that had once been rare and easily forgotten was now our default mode; grumpiness had become our new normal. This scared me, and rightly so; I'd always said I'd never be one of those wives, the kind that seethes quietly and avoids looking into her husband's eyes. When I started actively seeking the hidden significance of every questionable remark, looking for reasons to be mad, I knew it was time to make an adjustment.

That adjustment came on a warm summer morning, when Matthew was mowing the lawn and Poppy was sleeping. I was using the quiet time to clean the kitchen and to reflect a bit. Okay, not reflect. Worry.

I'm avoiding the big fights most of the time, I thought. *I'm keeping a positive outlook on Matthew's character, giving him the benefit of the doubt. And yet, the annoyance is still there; underneath it all, I'm still angry. How can I learn how to just let the little stuff go?*

I turned to the dishes, rinsing them hastily and placing them in the machine while watching Matthew out the front window. He was wrestling with the push mower, the one I opted to buy over the gas-powered kind, which meant that whatever went wrong with it would be my fault.

Here we go, I thought. *He seems frustrated. He's probably going to take it out on me.*

Unfortunately, the hasty assumption wasn't wrong.

Matthew let the mower fall from his outstretched

hands. Then he kicked it and stormed toward the house.

Unbeknownst to him, however, I was ready; in the seconds it took for him to get to the front door, I'd come up with a plan. Recalling my desire to reduce the annoyance that was clawing at us both, I decided that no matter what, I wouldn't overreact.

I wouldn't get defensive. I wouldn't make it a thing.

I would just let him be mad, and say nothing.

"Whatever possessed you to buy a manual mower?" Matthew said, predictably, entering the kitchen. "With our huge lawn, and all our pine trees? What a ridiculous waste of money that thing was. I'm getting rid of it. Today."

My internal reaction: bristling, hot-headed self-justification. My external reaction: do I flatter myself to say I was bemused? I didn't frown, didn't smile. I just looked at him and tilted my head. Maybe I raised my eyebrows, too.

Matthew paused a moment, waiting for the response that didn't come. Then he stormed down the hall to the TV room. I took a deep breath—one, then another. I was behaving well, but I was still upset.

Why is he blaming me for the lawn mower not working? I fumed. *He's being seriously irrational. He's taking something small then blowing it out of proportion at my expense. It makes me feel so disrespected.*

I placed the last dish in the machine. Then I went outside to retrieve the mower.

It looked as abandoned as I felt.

For the next half hour, I struggled through the tall grass, picking out the pine cones when they got stuck. As the lawn slowly improved in appearance, my sour mood shifted, too, and by the time I returned the mower to the garage, I had some perspective.

After washing up, I joined Matthew in the TV room and smiled at him over the screen.

"Don't let the lawn mower get the best of you, Hon," I said. Hearing this, Matthew's mood changed perceptibly.

"Thanks for finishing up," he said. And then he smiled. It was his way of apologizing, and I knew it.

What was I so worried about, anyway? I wondered. *My husband is wonderful, and he loves me. Yes, he was disrespectful. And emotional, and unfair.*

And he was also just being human.

―――

AFTER THAT NIGHT, and until Poppy was about nine months old, things were decidedly better between Matthew and I. Though we still argued regularly, and the ends to those arguments were more truces than resolutions, they were very welcome truces indeed. Sometimes, I even dared to hope our relationship was back to normal—or at least on its way to getting there.

I should've known this was just the beginning of the adventure.

And there was another, even greater consolation to be had, and that, of course, was the baby.

From the very first night—the very first moment, really—I just loved being a mother. I loved nursing. I loved cuddling. I loved long car rides and walks to nowhere. I loved staring at Poppy's face as she slept.

I loved that my job was loving.

Contrary to popular opinion, I told Genevieve, being a mom wasn't the hardest job on earth. If it weren't for the long hours and the sleep deprivation, it might've even been easy.

And so, even though I still remembered the hard times with Matthew that first year—the stress, the arguing, the frustration—it's not those feelings that come to mind first when recalling that time in my life.

Mostly, I remember my baby.

The baby's smile. Her dark curls. Her new discoveries, favorite songs. The way she drew admiring looks from total strangers wherever she went. The first time she sang, played with a ball, and didn't cry when Mom left.

And that's what Matthew remembers, too. He remembers falling in love.

Of course, the intensity of the experience of first motherhood wasn't all the good-feeling kind; particularly between the sixth and twelfth months, negative emotions ran high, too. Poppy hated babysitters, and being left alone, even for a moment. And getting her to sleep was still difficult. So, it wasn't that I didn't love the work.

It was just a whole lot of work.

One evening, the exhaustion caught up to me. Matthew was working late, so to kill time I took Poppy to the mall. In a seating area there I let Poppy "off the leash," so to speak, to explore the area as I rested. As the baby ran her hands over some scuffs on the floor, a woman stopped and stared at me in surprise.

"Aren't you afraid she'll get some horrible disease?" she asked.

And I very nearly lost my composure. To prevent a scene, I glared at her, saying nothing, until she took her disapproval elsewhere. Then I spent the next thirty minutes just trying to breathe.

Finally, it was time to meet Matthew for dinner. As expected, Poppy cried all the way home. When we arrived, I tried unsuccessfully to put her to sleep early, and when Matthew got home, later than expected, I had no tension left, only sadness.

"Hi, Hon. How was your evening?" Matthew asked as he poked his head into the bedroom.

I didn't even look at him.

"That rough, huh? What happened?"

I just shook my head. I could speak, but nothing in me wanted to.

Matthew took Poppy and started pacing the room, singing a song, while I curled up on the bed. Twenty minutes passed, and after Poppy finally drifted off, I was ready to tell him how I felt.

My voice was hushed to the point of unfamiliarity. "Why does she cry so much?" I asked.

"I don't know," Matthew said. "I'm sorry, Rachel. I love you."

It was the right response.

He put a hand on my shoulder, then put Poppy next to me and curled up on my other side. That night, whenever Poppy woke up, he picked her up and rocked her, allowing me to sleep without interruption.

It was the best sleep I'd had in months.

MY RELATIONSHIP JOURNAL: June
Lesson: Don't Make It Into a Big Deal

BOOK NOTES AND QUOTES:

TARA PARKER-POPE in *For Better: How the Surprising Science of Happy Couples Can Help Your Marriage Succeed*:

- Seventy percent of marital fights are

never resolved, even among happy couples.
- No two people agree on everything all the time, and to believe otherwise is unrealistic.

SHAUNTE FELDHAHN in *The Surprising Secrets of Highly Happy Marriages*:

- Most partners love their spouse more than their spouse realizes. In one survey, the overwhelming majority of people said that they "care deeply" about their partners, but only four in ten believed that their partners felt the same.
- Believing your partner loves you can help you believe the best about their intentions.

AARON BECK in *Love Is Never Enough: How Couples Can Overcome Misunderstanding*:

- While women often see talking about problems as a sign of a healthy relationship, men often believe the opposite: it's a sign that there are big problems.

MY RELATIONSHIP RESOLUTIONS:

- I won't overtalk. I won't discuss every nuance of our relationship with Matthew. Men love their dogs for a reason.
- I won't expect too much. Matthew has the right to a bad day, and so do I. We can apologize and move on.
- When something is bothering me a little

too much, I'll point it out nicely, once only, then drop the subject for a while. No big deal.
- I will continue to maintain close same-gender friendships, as well as hobbies that may or may not include Matthew. If Matt is my whole life, every disagreement threatens my happiness. I will not let this happen.
- Most important, I won't overreact, ever. In fact, I will under react. Even if at the time the problem seems like a big deal, I'll trust we'll figure it out eventually.

FOR THE FRIDGE:

- "I promise to under react."

5

Be Uncomfortably Nice

August came. Poppy was now seven months old, and though she was crying less often, she was still a handful. Fortunately, by this time, I'd mastered the routine that best served both our needs, and it started and ended with the car.

Poppy loved the car. In the morning, as soon as the crying started, I'd put her in her car seat and immediately, she'd quiet down. We'd drive to a store, to a play date, to a coffee shop—anywhere that would have us, really. While Poppy watched and learned, I shopped, chatted or read. Then came my favorite time of day: nap time. We'd head to the quiet road with no speed bumps and no stoplights, and twenty minutes later, she'd be down. I'd find a semi-secluded parking spot somewhere and read in the car. When Poppy woke up, there'd be another play date or a long walk. Then, a second nap, usually at home with me lying next to her, and by the time we woke up, Matthew would be home.

The days were long, but they were also indulgent; though I was often exhausted, I still felt lucky. And not only because I was spending the summer with my new baby, but because of a subtle shift happening with Matthew.

When Matthew and I first met, what he saw was a quiet woman with a strong will—someone who challenged him to be better, do more. What I saw in Matthew was something I needed just as much: a partner to truly have fun with. Matthew's philosophy of life was, enjoy and play. Mine was, work and work some more. In spite of this difference, though, our personalities blended well—so much so that until becoming parents, we hardly noticed the ways we didn't match up. Or maybe we did, but we knew that our differences were also strengths: I kept the train running down the track, and Matthew made sure we enjoyed the ride. 6'2"with a large build, Matt loved to play basketball, eat with abandon, throw dinner parties for his many friends. I, on the other hand, preferred working overtime at my paralegal job, then coming home to read or watch a movie.

Starting with my pregnancy, I brought my usual intensity to this parenting thing: I read all the books, tried the advice. After Poppy was born I kept a strict bedtime routine, carefully shielded her from computer screens, and narrated my day out loud to jump start her verbal skills.

Right from the start, though, Matthew was different. He sung to Poppy more, played silly games. He was goofy. He was lighthearted. When Poppy started solid food and threw it on the floor, he said, "If you keep doing that, I'm going to get you."

And this levity didn't just benefit Poppy—it was a huge asset to me, too. When Matthew finally arrived home from work after a long day, I felt a great sense of relief. It's true that he usually asked for dinner right away. But mostly he asked with a smile.

And that smile? It helped a lot.

Now, though, a change: as Poppy matured, Matthew's interactions with her did, too; this fun-loving dad was becoming a father. He spoke to Poppy about serious things long before she understood a word. He showed more interest in making decisions concerning her care—which shoes to buy, which foods to start her on, even which schools to consider for later. For the first time, he welcomed long nighttime discussions with me about all the pressing and not-so-pressing parenting matters.

Mostly, I enjoyed this. But not entirely.

The discussions brought us closer, I felt, and I loved knowing how much he cared. Every once in a while, though, we hit on a topic we couldn't agree on. And though I expected it would happen eventually, that didn't make it any less difficult. This was new territory for us, after all.

Our first big child-rearing disagreement, which I later called the Unfight, occurred as the summer was coming to an end. As the name suggests, the Unfight wasn't so much an argument as a tense discussion that could've turned personal, but didn't.

Which is why this time, it wasn't my failure that taught me my next great marriage lesson; instead, it was my success.

THE FIGHT WAS our most embarrassing one, occurring in a restaurant during a busy wedding celebration dinner. Almost as soon as we sat down, there was something between us, something we couldn't seem to shake. At first, little things got to us: Poppy's fussing in the high chair, throwing food, grabbing at our silverware. While I scolded gently, Matthew attempted bribe after bribe, pointing out that his technique was more successful. Poppy spilled her water, and interrupted every conversation, and by the time dinner came, I was ready to leave.

But of course, we could not leave.

Finally, dessert: peach pie and coffee. As the mood lightened, it happened: Matthew took a large forkful of the pie, and put it on Poppy's plate.

"Matthew!" I said, a little too loudly.

"Rachel. It's pie. It's a treat."

"I'm training her taste buds. You know how hard it is. It takes a lot of work to avoid unhealthy stuff."

"Well, maybe it's not worth it. Maybe it's okay to give in every once in a while. Maybe you're making your job too hard."

"Oh, you're blaming me now? For what? For trying to be a good parent? You're blaming me that raising a kid is so hard?"

I glared at Matthew. He glared back. Then I looked around, noticing the people that were noticing us. After picking Poppy's food scraps off of the floor and throwing them on the table, I escaped to the bathroom.

He breaks our rule, then embarrasses me about it? Wow. I can't believe that just happened. These were some of the thoughts that rushed to mind as I looked in the mirror and washed my hands. *How dare he say I make my job too hard, when he's the one who's making it so much harder? He acts like it's my choice that I'm stressed out about Poppy. If he helped me more, it'd be a lot easier.*

I took some deep breaths, then washed my face, and by the time I returned the check had been paid. My friends gave me sympathetic looks, then retreated to their cars. Matthew, though, was a little less well-mannered. We gathered up the baby and the baby supplies, and quietly walked out. On the way home, we got stuck in traffic.

I'm not going to stay mad, I'm not going to stay mad, I repeated to myself as the car slowed. *How can I act in this situation that will make me proud of myself afterward? How can I talk to him about it honestly, while still being nice?*

Immediately, I had my answer. It was all in the

tone of voice. That's what really mattered—not what I said.

Fucking eureka. I could say whatever I wanted, pretty much, as long as I used a respectful tone of voice.

Gathering scraps of sympathy for Matt, much as I'd gathered Poppy's leftovers, I took a deep breath and began.

"Matthew, I'm sorry I nagged you about the pie. I know you were just doing what you thought was best. I'm sorry if you thought I was accusing you of something."

Matthew turned his eyes from the traffic and looked directly at me. He relaxed a bit, giving me a forced smile. "It's not that you nagged me that I didn't like," he said. "It's that you always question my judgment. You try to make every decision about Poppy, and even when I have good ideas, you don't listen. You think you know everything and I know nothing."

"Really?" I asked. "But you don't tell me many ideas. I'm always the one who has to take charge."

"I don't need to give you input on every little thing. But when I do, you should know it's because it's something I care about."

I paused, taking this in. It made sense, actually. It wasn't about the nagging. It was about respect.

Matthew went on. "How many times have I given you good advice, and you just kept ignoring it till it was obvious I was right? Remember sleep training? You put it off for so long, and now you're so much more well-rested."

"That's true," I said. "You are often right. And it sounds like you don't think I know that. But Matthew, I do respect you. I know I'm a control freak and we don't always agree on everything but please don't ever question that. Okay?"

Matthew gave me a strange look, one I didn't quite recognize. Then, I did. It was emotion. He knew I was angry and was restraining that feeling in order to … well, to be nice. And he genuinely appreciated it.

For the rest of the ride home, we were quiet—quietly grateful. The argument had turned into a good thing. The pie, the no pie—that's not what this was about, we realized. It was about wanting to feel heard and loved.

Matt and I slept well that night. Then the following evening, after I'd thought it over a while, I decided to broach the subject—an uncomfortable one for Matthew—once again. I called him into the bedroom where I had been reading and told him I wanted to tell him something.

Matt stood in the doorway. "What is it?"

"You know, for everybody you love, the feeling is a little bit different," I said. "Some people, you have to work at it a bit. But with you, I've never had to. I've never had to convince myself of anything. Ever since we met, I just loved you. I love you as close to unconditionally as I am capable of—and nothing that has happened between us has ever changed that. Not the arguments and disagreements—nothing. Not even a little. You are just someone I truly like and love."

"Thank you, Rachel," Matthew said. "Thank you. Really. That's the nicest thing anyone has ever said to me."

"And I'm trying really hard to treat you this way, in a way that shows you this. I'm trying really hard every day."

"I know."

He sat on the bed next to me. "I love you, too. I really do. I'm sorry for the restaurant thing."

"It's okay."

"So our friends think we hate each other now, probably."

"It's fine. Just wait till they have kids. All judgment will be gone."

And that's how I learned my next important relationship lesson: it's not the words you say that matter most. What matters is that the other person feels cared about and respected—even in the middle of an argument.

What really matters is that you're nice.

My Relationship Journal: August
Lesson: Be Uncomfortably Nice

BOOK NOTES AND QUOTES:

JOHN GOTTMAN in *The Seven Principles for Making Marriage Work: A Practical Guide from the Country's Foremost Relationship Expert:*

- Three of the strategies for making marriage work are: enhance fondness and admiration, create shared meaning, and turn toward each other instead of away from each other.
- Cultivate habits that create mutual regard and that build trust.

TARA PARKER-POPE in *For Better: How the Surprising Science of Happy Couples Can Help Your Marriage Succeed*:

- The strongest marriages "… have at least a five-to-one daily ratio of positive to negative interactions."
- Don't just apologize to your spouse after mistreating them. Do or say five kind things to make up for it.

SUE JOHNSON in *Love Sense: The Revolutionary New Science of Romantic Relationships:*

- When a fight turns personal, it's usually because it isn't about the subject at hand; instead, it's about someone not feeling loved. An underlying, primal fear, such as the fear of abandonment, has been tapped.
- When you feel securely attached to your partner, you're more likely to discuss issues calmly, without the venom that characterizes a fight.
- For this reason, it's important to pay careful attention to the trust factor in your relationship ("Do I feel loved? Can I count on my partner to be there when I'm in need?"). It helps to create attachment rituals that you share with your partner throughout the day.

MY RELATIONSHIP RESOLUTIONS:

- I will remember that my partner's best motivation to help me with the kids and treat me well is my being kind, grateful and pleasant. Love begets love.
- I will compliment Matthew more often.
- I will say thank you more often,

particularly when I want Matthew to change a habit. ("Thanks for taking your shoes off at the door, Hon!")
- I will say "I love you" more often, and in a greater variety of ways.
- I will be consistently cheerful and respectful—even when Matthew is not.
- I will choose my words very, very carefully.
- I will use a kind tone of voice. Always.

FOR THE FRIDGE:

- "I promise to use a kind, respectful tone of voice, even when upset."

6

Shamelessly Bargain (And Always Have a Bottom Line)

Over the following few months as I continued to moderate my tone of voice and under react, Matthew instinctively followed my lead. Slowly, a beautiful shift in our relationship began: the big fights still happened, but the little ones largely subsided. This gave us an important relationship advantage: in between our fights, things were mostly back to normal. We had time to step back, to remind ourselves and each other that we'd be okay. It wasn't until the end of our first year we let that ability slip away—and when it did, it was hard to get it back.

As our ninth month of parenthood approached, not only were our relationship issues easier to handle —Poppy was a bit easier, too. No longer was the baby tethered to me every waking moment; now, she played on her own for minutes at a time, and as the year progressed the difference became even more pronounced. In addition, in September Matthew agreed to take her out at least twice a week, for at least two hours a session, giving my schedule some much-needed padding. He and Poppy came up with their own private mommy-free idea of fun, and for the first time since having the baby, Matthew experienced what I had appreciated about parenting all along: the addition of a brand new best friend. They went to the forest, to the zoo, to the play area at the mall—and Matthew enjoyed every minute. Then something happened that threw us off-balance once again, just as we had started to regain our footing.

That something was that I got a job.

The job was an excellent one—one that I enjoyed and that paid well. The timing was good, too; Poppy seemed ready for the occasional daycare adventure. Most important, the hours were perfect—about ten a week, and all from home. Matthew and I were confident we could transition smoothly.

We were wrong.

We were almost there, I thought as my work hours edged out much-needed rest and alone time. *We were almost back to normal. Or were we? Maybe the improvement I've been feeling lately was imagined—an illusion brought on by desperation and positive thinking.*

It was not a pleasant hypothesis to consider.

Soon after I started my job, the battles over our baby care schedule reasserted themselves. At first, they were mild ones, with most of the tension just beneath the surface. But as they became more frequent, their intensity increased as well, so that by fall they were bad.

If my first nine months of marriage with a child was about learning how to adjust my attitude toward Matthew—learning how to see him through eyes of love, not get angry at him and just be nice—the following year and a quarter was primarily a complement to that. It was about learning how to communicate better, to ask for what I wanted and to get it.

It was about actually solving our problems.

———

IF YOU HAD ASKED Matthew which of us was the source of the Great Birth Control Debate, he would almost certainly have said me. For weeks, even months on end, I chose to put off self-care, working long hours and multi-tasking instead. Looking back, I don't know why I allowed my workaholic side free rein for so long. Then again, most workaholics probably don't. At the time, however, Matthew was in a rare lull in his schedule. *Why can't he just pick up the slack?* I wondered.

Which is why, if you would have asked me which of us was the source of the Debate, I would almost certainly have said Matthew.

That October, Matthew's love of basketball had him either playing or watching television at least three evenings per week. He still took Poppy out on Sundays and Wednesdays, but Mondays, Fridays and Saturdays were booked up. On those days my long mornings and afternoons were followed by long, lonely evenings as well, which, of course, made me cranky. And not just because I wanted Matthew to take on more responsibilities, but because I wanted to just be with him. I wanted to take walks together, have dinner with friends, go to the zoo.

I wanted to feel like a family.

And so, one day in the midst of this predicament, I decided I couldn't take it anymore. I made an announcement—an ultimatum, really, and one I intended to keep: "If you don't stop prioritizing your fun stuff over the family, I am going back on birth control."

The news did not go over well.

It was around midnight, after Poppy had gone to bed, and though I was tired I told Matthew I'd hang out. We were sitting on the living room couch, evaluating lackluster movie options, my head resting comfortably on his shoulder. The month prior, after a year and a half of menstruation-free breastfeeding, my period had finally returned, necessitating a reproduction-related decision. First, I made an appointment with my doctor. Then I told Matthew the plan.

"Hon, there's something I've been thinking about that I need to tell you, and you're probably not going to like it very much," I said.

And then I delivered the blow.

Matthew's first response was to freeze, TV remote in midair. Then he just shook his head. "No, you're not," he told me.

"I already made the appointment." I moved my body away from him, backing into the couch's arm rest. Then I curled my legs against my chest with my arms.

"Without even telling me?" Matthew threw down the remote. "Why would you do such a thing?"

"Matthew, you know why. I'm so stressed. I'm so exhausted. I just can't do this the way I have been lately."

"Rachel, we had a plan. The same plan we've had all along."

"I know, Hon, I know. I'm sorry. But what's happening right now with your sleep schedule—it's not fair. It's not right. I'm just feeling so cheated."

"So that's why you're doing this. To get back at me. I see."

"No, that's not the reason—really. It's not just what's going on right now. It's how things have been all along. It's been hard. Harder than you know."

I continued. "We have Poppy, and I'm so glad we do. Having her has only made me want our second even more. But it doesn't have to happen right now. We have time. It's only been a year, after all. Our kids can be spaced a bit more."

"So you're just making a threat rather than discussing it? Typical. That's always what you do."

"No. I've been trying to discuss it. I've been trying for a long time. There are little changes, but it's not enough. One kid is already so difficult for us; I'm not going to do this with two. That's just not the choice I'm going to make."

"You know what I'm going to say, don't you?"

"That I'm making things harder than they have to be? That I work too much? Well, why don't you do more so I don't have to?"

"I do work. I work a lot. But when I need time, I take it."

"We're going in circles now, like we always do. Maybe we'll figure this out. But until we do, I don't want to get pregnant."

With that, the arguing ended; Matthew and I went our separate ways. But the fight definitely wasn't over. For the next few days, a sort of suburban cease-fire was silently declared: we avoided each other most of the time, and avoided serious discussion entirely. This gave us time to think about what to do next, to weigh our advantages and to strategize. In international relations and in married life, however, eventually someone has to make a move.

This time, that someone was Matthew.

A few days after the argument, he offered to take Poppy out for the evening. He said they were going to dinner, but by the time they got back three hours had passed.

When they returned home, Matthew greeted me with a smile. "When is your doctor appointment?" he asked.

"Not till next week," I replied. "Why do you ask?"

The following day, Matthew took Poppy to the park, and soon after that, he started taping his games to watch after I went to bed. For my part, I hired a babysitter to cover one evening per week. I called my doctor and canceled my birth control appointment, and three months later, I was pregnant.

The pregnancy was, of course, the most significant result of the Great Birth Control Debate. However, there was another worth mentioning, too. One evening a week or so after the fight, we sent Poppy to a friend's house and sat down at the dining room table, pen and paper at hand.

Then we began negotiations.

We went through each day of the week, section by section, and decided who'd be responsible for what. Who would make dinner? Who would clean the car? When would we both exercise? Who'd get to sleep in, and on which days, and what about weekends when I was working? For the first time since becoming parents, we decided to be deliberate about our schedule, taking all of our needs—not just work and sleep—seriously.

Finally, we decided to stop winging it.

Here is a list of all of the chunks of time we thought through together, plus a list of all of the important activities we included in our new family schedule.

Baby Care Scheduling Considerations:

- Weekday mornings
- Weekday work times
- Weekday dinnertime
- Weekday evenings after dinner
- Weekday bedtimes
- Weekday overnights
- Saturday early mornings
- Saturday late mornings
- Saturday afternoons
- Saturday dinnertime
- Saturday evenings after dinner

- Saturday overnights
- Sunday early mornings
- Sunday late mornings
- Sunday afternoons
- Sunday dinnertime
- Sunday evenings after dinner
- Sunday overnights

Activities to Include in the Family Schedule:

- Paid work time for Dad
- Paid work time for Mom
- Transportation time for parents
- Transportation time for children
- Cooking time
- Cleaning time
- Meal times
- Recreational time for children
- Educational time for children
- Exercise time for Mom
- Exercise time for Dad
- Alone time for Dad
- Alone time for Mom
- Date nights for parents
- Mom's time with friends
- Dad's time with friends
- Family time at home
- Family outings
- Mom's one-on-one time with each child
- Dad's one-on-one time with each child
- Mom's household management time
- Dad's household management time
- Time for home maintenance and repairs
- Time for special activities and projects

- Adequate sleep time for each family member

IT WAS QUITE a conversation we had that evening—and the schedule we agreed upon, no small feat. In creating it, I wanted a guarantee of some kind—a way to ensure Matthew would give me the breaks I needed. For his part, Matthew hoped for more predictability, a way to ensure he wouldn't be endlessly nagged to do more.

Our hopes were ridiculously high. However, more important than the schedule itself was the fact that we created it at all. In doing so I expanded my relationship skill set considerably.

I learned how to negotiate—and shamelessly.

Marriage is transactional, I realized as we made our plan. It's not always romantic, and that's okay. If he doesn't want to do something I want him to do, it's not because he's a jerk or doesn't love me. It's because he has needs, too.

My Relationship Journal: September
Lesson: Shamelessly Bargain (And Always Have a Bottom Line)

BOOK NOTES AND QUOTES:

WILLARD HARLEY, JR. in *His Needs, Her Needs: Building an Affair-Proof Marriage:*

- Marriage is transactional. "The more you give to your partner, the more they give to you."

- Couples have an "inner scoring device you probably never realized you had" that the author calls a Love Bank. Somewhere deep inside our (mathematically skilled) subconscious, we're keeping track of each others' balances, and we understand when we're due payment, and when we owe. When the giving is roughly equal and both partners get their needs met, the relationship is satisfactory to both. When there's unequal giving, though, the marriage runs into trouble—if not right away, then eventually. The goal, then, is to ensure your transactions even out as much as possible so that neither partner ever feels cheated.

NEALE DONALD WALSCH in *Neale Donald Walsch on Relationships:*

- Relationships don't have to be a friendly (or not-so-friendly) game of tug of war. When disagreements arise and neither partner is willing to compromise, offering clear consequences takes care of the problem. An example: If one day your partner suddenly decides to take up smoking, and you aren't okay with that, you don't have to yell or nag. The solution is simple: You tell your partner that you love and respect them, but if they keep smoking in your home you'll have to move out.

FOSTER CLINE AND JIM FAY in *Parenting With Love and Logic:*

- Many parenting skills apply to other relationships, too, including friendship and marriage.
- Effective parents don't use anger, nagging and threats; instead, they offer choices. When kids try to argue, they don't engage; instead, they say "I understand," then repeat the choice.
- Some examples of choices effective parents give: "Are you planning to be unkind for a while? If so, I'm going to spend some time away from you." "If you hit, you lose." "If you spend your allowance on something else, I won't be able to pay your phone bill for you."

MY RELATIONSHIP RESOLUTIONS:

- I won't over-romanticize marriage. My husband isn't going to do whatever I want him to do just because he loves me; there has to be something in it for him, too. By the same token, I won't be embarrassed to admit when I'm doing something for him in order to get something in return. Doing so is just part of my self-care.
- When something isn't working for me, I won't nag. I'll negotiate. I'll communicate my needs clearly and allow him to do the same.
- During negotiations, I'll focus on solutions, not emotions. No anger. No accusations. No spinning off into fear. Instead, I will simply describe what I want, then discuss the matter till it's resolved.
- I will have clear and reasonable

expectations. I will know what I really need from Matthew and what I'm willing to compromise on or give up.
- I will have clear consequences. If Matthew doesn't follow through on an agreement, I will look for a way he can make it up to me.
- I will always have a bottom line. If Matthew doesn't agree to giving me a certain amount of money or a certain amount of alone time, I will take it anyway and let him choose to either remain angry or accept it.
- I will keep my end of the bargain.
- I will demand a fair transaction. I won't stay in an unhealthy relationship. I am not a martyr.
- Most of all, I will remember to keep it simple. Relationships are hard—some of the time. But with clear communication, clear expectations and clear consequences, most of the time, they should feel pretty easy the rest of the time.

FOR THE FRIDGE:

- "I promise to negotiate, not nag."
- "I promise to focus mainly on solutions, not emotions."

7

Apologize Every Chance You Get

Taken separately, most of the first-year fights Matthew and I had weren't terribly significant; it was their accumulation that was the problem. As year two of parenthood began, though, the intensity increased and our recovery times did, too.

The First Trimester Tussle was one of our worst arguments of all time, and it was largely my fault. In addition to the apparent cause was the underlying one, namely: I was pregnant. And I was miserable. I was miserable in a way I hadn't been in years, before the baby, before ever meeting Matthew. Exhaustion, nausea, lower back spasms: my pregnancy pain cocktail tasted terrible. I even felt pregnant in my sleep.

My sixth week in, I gave up exercise. My seventh, I gave up healthy eating. By my ninth week, depression had fully set in, and everything was difficult, even conversation. Other than the requisite life management stuff and bare civilities, most of the words that exited my mouth were complaints.

Towards the end of that three-month period, myself, Matthew and Poppy went to my hometown to visit my family. Under normal circumstances, it would've been a happy occasion full of old favorites: favorite hotel, favorite restaurants, favorite scenic drives. This time, though, I dragged through the routines, and for some reason Matthew was nearly as sullen. And so, on the second night, as he and I lay in the hotel bed, I attempted some perfunctory compassion.

I asked Matthew what was wrong.

"Do you really want to know?" Matthew asked, placing his hand on my foot.

"Yes," I said. "I really do."

"Okay. Well, Hon, I'm sick of your complaining."

Deep breath. In, then slowly out. In, then out again. Anger, sadness. Anger, guilt. Anger. Sadness. Deep breath.

"Okay," I said. "So you don't want me to talk about anything I'm feeling, what I'm going through? Is that it?"

"It's just too much," Matthew said, rubbing my foot. "I feel like I can't take it anymore." The only thing that saved us from the inevitable full-scale fight that night was that he said it nicely.

"But I'm trying," I said. "I really, really am. You have no idea what this is like."

"I know. But the complaining—does it help? Does it actually make you feel better? I don't think it does. I think it makes it worse."

I didn't answer; instead, I turned my body away, loosening my foot from his hand. After several minutes, Matthew turned on the TV and found an old movie to watch. When it ended, he turned off the TV, then adjusted his pillow.

In the dark, I turned back towards him, then put his hand on my stomach. I held it there and rubbed it a bit.

"I'll try harder," I said in just-above-whisper volume. "I won't complain so much anymore."

It was a promise I didn't keep for long.

The following day, Matthew returned home and went back to work, while Poppy and I stayed on. I hoped that the last two days would be better than the first, but it was not to be: they were worse. By the time the trip was over and I met Matthew at the airport, I wasn't at my breaking point; I'd already slightly cracked.

"How did it go?" Matthew asked, greeting me with a kiss. Anger filled me. *As if he cares. He doesn't want to hear about it, and I told him I wouldn't complain. There's nothing I can do but lie or say nothing.*

I shook my head. "I don't want to talk about it."

He gave me a grim look and took one of my bags, then led me down the long hallway to the door. *One moment down, a million more to go*, I thought. And it wasn't long before there was another.

"You're quiet," Matthew said as we left the terminal. "Did something happen after I left?"

Hmm …, I thought. *He knows I'm mad, but he asked anyway. Points for that. I'll try to calm down.*

"Well, I'm not allowed to talk about it, am I?" I replied. *Okay, that didn't sound as nice as I'd hoped it would.*

"I don't know, Hon," Matthew said. "Maybe not. I don't know."

It was not the right answer.

As soon as we got in the car I turned my face to the window, trying to hold myself together. By the time we exited the parking garage, though, I couldn't stand it any longer; I spoke.

"After you left, my dad yelled at me, which pretty much ruined the rest of the trip. On the way to the airport, I got a speeding ticket. And the rental car company was closed when I got there so I couldn't figure out how to return the car and we almost missed our plane. It was horrible."

Matthew could've let it go. He could've given me

some leeway. Instead, he sighed. "Hon. You didn't even make it one hour."

Second crack. Tears. Third crack. Shaking and sobs. Several minutes of this, and I felt shattered. The screaming that followed came not from my throat, but from somewhere much deeper inside.

THE FIRST TRIMESTER Tussle wasn't a single-day affair—not by a very long shot. The yelling lasted hours. The sarcasm, days. And the anger lasted nearly a month.

During this time, my terrible night thoughts visited regularly. And their themes were familiar. *I can't believe he actually said that,* the narrative began. *Can't he even pretend to feel compassion? I'm pregnant, sick and hormonal, but I still have to be the strong one; he's not picking up the slack.*

Well, I'm stuck, now. Especially after having kids. That's great. My life is ruined.

One night, feeling helpless against my inner rage, I made a healthy decision.

I called Gen.

"I've been mad at Matthew for a solid month," I said.

"Yeah?" she said. "Tell me about it."

"He's been doing his stuff–his stuff with Poppy– the schedule stuff I told you about. But there's this … undercurrent. I can't forget the fight. At least, not for very long. I don't know what to do. Do we go to counseling? Or do I just assume this is pregnancy hormones and it'll pass?"

"Well, the fight was bad," Gen said. "It might take a while to get over and you can't expect to feel great mentally right now. I don't know, Rachel. Marriage is so hard. It's just hard to deal with another person all the time, even when you're trying your absolute best. The good news is, most of this stuff you'll forget soon enough. Probably much sooner, and much more thoroughly, than you think."

As I considered this, she went on. "Do you even remember what your last few fights were about? The small ones, not the big ones."

"No."

"What about a big fight that happened several months ago?"

"I guess not. Not right now, no."

"I know you already apologized, Rachel. And I know you want Matthew to do the same. But he might not. And that's okay. Sometimes, you just have to be the apologizer. Play that role. You'd be surprised how much it will help and how much will be forgotten. As for the emotions, they're going to be there sometimes. My advice? Just put your head down and get through it."

And so, that is what I did. I apologized to Matthew again for my moodiness and anger, even though I felt doing so was unnecessary, even unfair. I reminded myself how much my hormones were affecting me lately.

I put my head down, and got through it.

THE FIRST TIME Matthew and I had a real fight—not a disagreement, but a fight—was a full six months into our relationship. We were cleaning his house to make room for my things for my planned move-in, date TBD.

It had been a long day, and both of us were tired. Not tired—exhausted. Spent. Then, it happened. Matthew handed me a heavy box from a high shelf, and as I set it down, an unmistakable sound: breaking glass.

"What was it?" I asked, already using the past tense.

Matthew didn't answer. He grabbed the box. When he opened it, we assessed the damage. A rook from his chess set was chipped and a bishop was missing a knob.

That could've been worse, I thought.

Matthew saw it differently.

"Where was the bubble wrap?" he asked. "You were the one who packed this, right?"

"I guess ... I guess I ran out."

"You ran out? Well, when we run out, we get more. We don't just pack stuff like this without bubble wrap."

I didn't respond.

Matthew closed the box and set it on his desk. Then he returned to the shelf. When I took my spot next to him, though, he shook his head at me.

"You are not allowed touch my stuff anymore," he said.

"Hey, Matt," I said, my defensiveness turning to anger. "Wait a second. Think about this. I've spent the last two days cleaning this place—packing stuff, donating stuff, cleaning your kitchens and your bathrooms. I did way more than you did, so don't you dare get an attitude with me about this. It was an accident, okay?"

It was the first time I ever raised my voice to Matthew. And it was certainly the first time I walked away in anger. I left the room, slamming the door, then left the house, slamming that door, too. Then I went for a walk.

Five minutes passed—a very long five minutes. It was the first fight of newly-in-loves, after all. We were still convinced everything was perfect between us ... and at the same time, afraid it wasn't.

Soon, I heard footsteps. Someone was running up behind me. I turned around, and there he was.

It was Matthew.

And in the time that it took me to recognize him, and the look of apology on his face, my anger disappeared completely.

I stopped walking, and Matthew caught up to me, then gave me a long, loving hug.

"I'm sorry," he said. "You're right. I should've helped you more."

"I'm sorry, too. I should've been more careful with your stuff." The apology wasn't sincere—not completely, anyway. But it felt like the right thing to say.

We hugged some more, then kissed, then walked back to the house together. And that was it.

It was over.

Apologies are awesome, I realized after talking to Matthew about the First Trimester Tussle. *They're, like, the fastest relationship cure ever. They get you out of a bad spiral, help you reset. And sometimes, that's all you need—just a reset button.*

You don't even have to mean it all the time.

———

My Relationship Journal: February
Lesson: Apologize Every Chance You Get

BOOK NOTES AND QUOTES:

SUE JOHNSON in *Hold Me Tight: Seven Conversations for a Lifetime of Love*:

- Humans are hardwired for love and

connection. Our need for our spouse isn't a weakness, but a strength: securely attached people are more confident and more successful.
- Part of securely attaching to your partner is honoring their feelings and, when in the wrong, apologizing. This should be done in the context of a conversation in which the couple fully discusses the nature of the wrongdoing, the feelings that were hurt and a reestablishing of trust.

ECKHART TOLLE in *A New Earth: Awakening to Your Life's Purpose:*

- Due to our ego, we're constantly seeking approval from others. This seeking leads to resentment when any kind of disagreement—often even a minor one—occurs. So, get rid of ego. It's just not helping. All that anger, defensiveness, arguing, making wrong, being right ... all of that can safely go away. The death of your ego is not the death of you. Instead, it's the start of your real life.
- Don't just get rid of your own ego, though: stop reacting to the ego in others. This is the most effective way to not only avoid arguments, but to actually dissolve the other person's anger and bring back their sanity. Then real communication can begin.

MY RELATIONSHIP RESOLUTIONS:

- I will take every opportunity to apologize.

I will humbly ask for forgiveness, and generously forgive myself.
- I will remember that my ego isn't my friend. It causes me to interpret every confrontation as a potential threat, and makes me defensive.

FOR THE FRIDGE:

- "I promise to take every opportunity to apologize."

8

Change Your Partner the Right Way

After the First Trimester Tussle, I promised I'd forgive myself. And I did—but that didn't solve everything. Though in my second three months of pregnancy my nausea and discomfort decreased significantly, the unease I felt about my marriage lingered.

Matthew and I were still treading water.

In the months following the argument, we stuck to our child care schedule. Yet no matter how fair things seemed on the surface, I couldn't shake the feeling something was missing. Matthew was doing his part. He was taking Poppy out, helping with the cleaning. I could do my work without interruption. But he was withdrawn. He was distant. He watched the clock, checked the boxes.

He was just doing his duty.

Which is part of the reason that in late March, just two months after our worst fight ever, we had another that was nearly as bad.

It happened because of the dishes. Well—not just the dishes, maybe, but the dishes as well as my repeated requests for Matthew to take care of them. One evening, before doing what I thought of as a favor to him–taking Poppy to an art class for two hours during his scheduled Poppy time—I repeated my request yet again.

"The dishes, Hon, the dishes. They're really getting bad. Can you do at least some of them while we're gone?"

Matthew gave me a grim look and did not respond, so I sighed, packed a diaper bag and left with Poppy. I enjoyed our outing, but when I returned later that night, the dishes were still in the sink ... and Matthew was on the couch watching TV.

Seeing this, anger. Waves, like before. *I'm getting tired of this. I need a boat already. Where is it?*

I didn't find a boat that night. But I did find a log to grab onto—one just big enough to give me a short rest. Rather than mentioning my disappointment to Matthew, starting an argument I couldn't win, I asked him to take Poppy out the following evening.

He agreed. I was relieved. But the following night, just before he walked out the door, he called something over his shoulder.

"Can you do the dishes while we're gone?"

I didn't reply, but he didn't wait for me to, anyway. I heard footsteps, then a purposeful bang. Matthew had closed the door and left without saying goodbye, something that he knew I hated.

My first response: *Gut check. Wow. That was rude. Why would he shut the door on me like that? Is he mad at me for asking him to do the dishes last night? How petty. Now we're in a fight, and for what?*

That evening at the restaurant, Matthew and Poppy dined on thick fries and a thicker steak, but home alone, I didn't eat much. The meal I'd planned and the book I'd selected were postponed for another day and I lay in bed and wallowed instead. When Matthew returned, I decided once again to break my own rule.

I started an argument at night.

And it was bad. It was bad for all the reasons sudden nighttime fights are usually bad—uncontrollable emotion due to exhaustion and the freshness of the wound. Added to that, though, was the built-up resentment that I'd been unable to let go of for so long.

Simply put: I was out of control.

The scene went something like this: Matthew and Poppy got home. When they found me in bed, Matthew gave me the baby. With glazed-over eyes, I took Poppy and started to nurse. Then I started in on Matthew.

"It was my first night off in a week, and you left in a huff. How could you be so rude to me, Matt?"

"All I did was what you did, just the night before. You asked me to do the dishes on my night off."

"Your night off? That was my night. I gave that one to you. And the dishes wouldn't've taken the whole time."

"But the dishes are your chore. They've always been your chore. It's like now that I'm doing more with Poppy, your standards have just gotten even higher. You want me to start taking on more of the housework and you're nagging me about it every day. I'm sticking to the schedule. How much more will you want from me?"

"The dishes are my chore? I don't think so." I got out of bed and set the baby on the floor. I was shaking.

Here, we rehashed our chore breakdown in detail, as well as our evening schedule. Twenty minutes of shouting later, we still differed in our perspectives. While Matthew felt I should take on the responsibility alone, I thought we should each wash what we used.

"Anyway," I concluded, "This isn't just about the dishes. It's about how rude you were to me. You walked out on me, angry. You ruined my night. You really need to apologize for that."

"Apologize? Not a chance. You should apologize. You're the one who's nagging me all the time."

"And why wouldn't I? If I don't, you conveniently 'forget' what we're doing that night. I have to practically beg you to keep your agreements."

"Hey, that's not fair. I would do it without being reminded. You just never give me a chance to."

"Fine, Matthew, I'm sorry. I know I've been nagging. I just don't know what else to do."

"How about not being such a control freak? You barely talk to me except to ask me to help you with something. I get less grief from my boss."

"When do I even see you? When do we have time for a conversation? You're working all the time. You won't even take all your vacation."

"And you continue to make things harder on yourself, Rachel. You still don't take naps. You still won't get a babysitter so we can go out together."

"You know how much work it is to find a babysitter? Oh, no, you don't—you've never done it."

"Well, it's not as if I'm not doing other things. Ever since making our schedule, we've stuck to it. What more do you want from me?"

"I don't know."

I sat. I took a deep breath. "I don't know, Matt. I don't know. I want you to be nice, even when you're in a bad mood. I want you to want to clean the house and be with Poppy, even when you don't absolutely have to."

"You want to change me."

"Yes, I guess I do."

"Thanks, Rachel. Thanks a whole lot."

"No, Matt, that's not what I meant. I meant … I don't know what I meant. I really just want to be a loving, happy family."

"Well, then, we have to spend family time together. But when? With you working and me taking Poppy out all the time? Is there even time?"

I picked up Poppy and held her to my breast again. She nuzzled into my chest.

"I don't know."

THE DAY after the Dish Debacle I got up earlier than usual. I cleaned, cooked and played with Poppy, pretending everything was fine.

But that did not make it fine.

In the afternoon, I took Poppy to the park to meet Gen and Max. Knowing that between snacks, diaper changes and "Mom, come push me on the swing!" we wouldn't have long to chat, as soon as we found a bench and the kids scampered off, I jumped right in.

"Matt and I had a fight. Another bad one. I'm not even sure what it was about. Housework?"

"Oh, one of those. Housework. Such a catalyst."

"Yeah. I apologized, but it's like, 'I'm sorry I nagged you. Can you do the dishes?'"

Gen laughed.

"And then it was about our schedule, and me feeling like he doesn't care enough about the family, and all the rest of it, yada yada."

"Aww, I'm sorry, Rachel. That sucks."

"I know. It does."

"So do you really think he doesn't care enough about you? Or … what's the real problem here?"

"I don't, but I do. I don't know. Gen, you almost never complain about your marriage. Why is that? Have I ever asked you? If I haven't, let me correct that error now."

"I don't think you have, Rachel. And I don't

know the answer. Maybe it's all about having clear expectations. Who does what and when, and all that."

"Yeah, that's good, and that's what Matthew and I have been doing, too. Ever since making our schedule. Still, I'm starting to wonder if its really the right thing for us. I can't quite explain it, but it feels like something's missing."

"Well, has he been doing his part every day? And how does he do it? Is he dragging his feet?"

"Yes, he's sticking to it, and so am I, pretty carefully—and it's been several months now, so I feel good about that. But to your other question, yes, he does drag his feet. And then I end up nagging.

"And I really, really hate nagging. Not only because it's thin-ice territory for him, and tends to make him grumpy, but because it makes me feel unloved. I start wondering why he won't just do his part without my asking first as a way to show me he cares. Then we're both in a bad mood.

"Sometimes I think we're just planning everything too much. Why can't he just look out for me, and me for him? Why does it have to be so complicated?"

"Well, it's complicated because everything is complicated. He wants to look out for you, but he has to look out for himself, too. I mean theoretically, if you both put the other person first all the time, both of you would get your needs met. But relationships just don't work that way. So get that idea out of your mind right now. Lose that expectation. His main job in life is to take care of himself. And so is yours."

"Yikes," I said. "That's hard to hear."

"Is it? Would you really want the job of making him happy? If he left you in charge of taking care of him, how would you make that happen? Would you just do everything he asked you to do? What about when what you wanted didn't line up with what he wanted? Who wins? Do you each fight for what the other wants? Anyway, how would you even know what he wanted in the first place?"

"Okay. I see that. Okay."

"Your husband is not going to put you first all of the time. Some of the time, but not all. Won't happen," Gen said.

"I get it."

"But yeah, it's complicated. And it's going to stay that way. It's hard enough when there are just two people's needs to consider, but now there are three of you. That said, you could probably simplify things a bit."

"How?"

"When I was pregnant with Max, Richard and I made an agreement. Since he was our third I knew that my alone time was basically over, at least until the kids were in school. So instead of trying to figure out an exact schedule to make it work, I told him that all I really wanted was for him to be present with us after he got home from work, pitching in and doing what he could until all the kids were in bed."

"Wow. And what was that like?"

"Honestly?" Genevieve said. "It was the best thing ever. Before that, we were doing what you guys are doing—planning our evenings and weekends in advance as much as possible. But, well, it never quite felt fair. I was always the default parent, the one on duty when nothing else was negotiated. After that one discussion, our marriage really changed. It became more of a partnership.

"We still go by that guideline most days of the week, and a lot of the weekend, too. When Richard comes home, he plays with the kids while I get dinner, and we take turns with chores and bedtime stuff.

It's good for all of us, really. Even Richard can't imagine it any other way. He's gotten used to being together as a family every evening."

"That sounds awesome," I said. "But do you think Matt would go for something like that? It would be such a big change."

"But he's already doing a lot. Maybe he'd rather not be on quite as strict of a schedule. Maybe he misses your laid-back, unscheduled time, too."

"Maybe. Or maybe our expectations would get fuzzy again, and I'd be nagging even more than before."

"You never know. You might be surprised."

"If it worked, I would be. It would feel like a coup. Like something fundamental changed in Matthew's personality. And you know what people say about trying to change your partner."

"What? That it's not possible? They're wrong."

"What?"

"Oh, Rachel. We all change our partners, all of the time."

"How? What do you mean?"

"People change, in small ways, to reflect your expectations of them. And even more so in marriage. A lot of the time, what you think you'll get is what you get. They can sense it and they find themselves acting how you think they'll act."

"So have I changed Matthew?"

"What do you think?"

"Hmm ... yeah, I think I have. One of the first things I learned after having Poppy was to change my stories about him—to see the best in him. After that, I noticed a big change: he was less moody. Then we both learned how to talk instead of getting emotional about everything right away. I think he followed my lead on that one, too. He still doesn't always apologize, and he still does hurtful things, but whenever I'm in a good mood, he's much more likely to be pleasant, too. The other day I was feeling really positive and he picked up on that. He sent me a text that said, 'I love you.'"

"That's cute."

"I know. And he doesn't do that stuff just to make me feel good. He only does it when he's really feeling that way."

"Richard, too. So it sounds like what you're saying is that Matt has changed for the better, but not from nagging. Mostly from just improving your attitude."

"I don't know. Maybe. Maybe nagging helps a bit, too. There are times when I think it has."

"But nagging nicely. Nagging gently, and not all the time."

"Yeah. It's a different kind of nag. More light-hearted."

With that, an interruption. First one, then a cascade. Max needed to use the bathroom, then both kids needed food and water. When the dominoes stopped falling, I picked up where we left off.

"So basically, Gen, what you're telling me is that at times I can change Matt by expecting the best of him, and other times I can either learn how to nag in a nice way or have a well-planned, respectful conversation?"

"I might have said all that, yeah. Worth a try anyway. Can't hurt to try. Won't work with everything, but you might be surprised. Package it well. Show him the benefits. Most of the time, what you want is what will make him happy, too."

THAT NIGHT, after Matthew came home, I popped some popcorn—his favorite snack—and we sat in the family room and discussed our relationship yet again.

"I know things have been rough for the past couple of months," I told him. "And I'm sorry for not holding it together a bit better. I've been picking fights and hurting you, and I really don't want to do that anymore."

Matthew looked at me gratefully. *He's easy to soften,* I realized. *It takes such a small gesture. An apology. A loving touch. Even a smile will often do the trick. Why don't I do this more?*

"I talked to Gen today and told her a little about this, and she made a really good suggestion. She said that she thinks our schedule has been great, but that we might need a bit more flexibility. How would you feel about both of us working together in the evenings, instead of taking turns like we have been? I don't want to be co-workers, watching the clock all the time, taking things in shifts. I want us to be more like partners."

"Interesting," Matthew replied. "That actually makes sense. We discuss each night what we need to get done, or just spend the evening hanging out together."

"Exactly."

"Hmm … Yeah. We could try it."

In the years to follow, I would know the true significance of this conversation. That evening, though, I only suspected it. I took another bite of popcorn and when Poppy held out her hand, put a few kernels in it. As I looked at her face, then at Matthew's, a deep love for them came over me—as well as a great feeling of relief.

It's true, I thought, *I don't need Matthew to always take care of me or put me first. I can do that. But I do need him to be there.*

My Relationship Journal: April
Lesson: Change Your Partner the Right Way

BOOK NOTES AND QUOTES:

KIRA ASATRYAN, relationship coach, in an article on PsychologyToday.com:

- Model the changes you want to see in your partner. This works partly because we tend to mirror people around us, and partly because knowing what you should do is more powerful than knowing what you shouldn't do.
- Show your partner that you're changing in ways that matter to them, too.

DAN SAVAGE on StarTalkRadio.net:

- It's possible to sand off some of your partner's imperfections, but there are things, too, that you will never change. These qualities are what Savage refers to as "the price of admission."
- "And you have to ask yourself, Is this person worth paying the price of admission to put up with that? And not put up with it and complain about it and guilt them about it all the time, put up with it and shut up about it."

MY RELATIONSHIP RESOLUTIONS:

- I will figure out exactly what I want to change about my partner and our

relationship. This can be harder than it seems.
- I will determine whether or not I can help my partner make the change. Sweeping character alterations aren't my territory. Changes of habit, schedules and circumstances might be.
- I will only seek one big change at a time. This helps me clarify my needs, limit nagging and manage my expectations.
- I will learn the art of the "slow nag." Once I have a clear, main objective, rather than using the classic nagging technique—whine and repeat—I will use compliments, detached observations and jokes to good-naturedly encourage the change I want to see. Occasionally, a polite direct request will also do. An example of a detached observation: "That guy just bashed his wife to his friends. What a loser." A joke: "You little stinker! Get your stinky butt out of bed!" And a direct request: "I really prefer it when you use a polite tone of voice when asking me to do something."
- Occasionally, after the slow approach hasn't worked, I'll use the confrontation method. During the confrontation I'll use "I feel" and "lately it seems" statements, rather than "you are" and "you always" statements. I will focus on problems and solutions rather than perceived character flaws.
- I will change, too. And talk about it with my partner.
- I will be patient. People do change. People do grow. If I continue to expect

the best of my husband, he will continue to move in that general direction (albeit rather slowly sometimes).
- I'll accept the things I cannot change about Matthew, even after four thousand super polite hints and conversations.

FOR THE FRIDGE:

- "I promise not to nag you to change, but to gently encourage it instead."

MY RELATIONSHIP RESOLUTIONS:

- I will make Matthew's alone time a priority.
- I will give myself time-outs when I need them, too.
- I will communicate clearly. I won't wait for Matthew to offer breaks, compliments, words of appreciation or anything else; instead, I will ask him for them.
- I will focus on solutions, not emotions. This is an easier kind of conversation for men to have.
- I will talk about my feelings with my female friends more often than I do with my husband.
- I will avoid the temptation to compare lives. Sure, the number of hours I work is higher than the number Matthew works. But I get to play with Poppy and spend time with friends. He has to go to an office. With a boss.

FOR THE FRIDGE:

- "I promise to focus on solutions, not emotions."

10

Don't Defend Yourself

I was learning. Matthew was learning. And yet, we had a long way to go; that much was clear to both of us. As we rounded the Year Three corner, another obstacle greeted us, though looking back, I'm not sure why it did, exactly. Was it because after two years of on-and-off tension we'd forgotten how to be comfortably in love? Was it because having solved several seemingly insurmountable problems, we were now expecting—even looking for—another?

Had we made annoyance a habit?

Whatever the origin of our latest issue, its nature was readily apparent: little mistakes or missteps were blown out of proportion, like tiny relationship land mines. When I repeatedly left the front door open while carting stuff to and from the car, Matthew furiously pointed out all the insects. When Matthew slipped his shoes off near the door, leaving them directly in my path, I picked them up and threw them across the room. When I scratched the car, Matthew was sarcastic and rude, and when Matt didn't answer his cell phone, I sent him an angry text. In short: One of us would be annoying, and the other would get annoyed. Nothing too dramatic, but we needed a different coping mechanism.

Of course, there were the bigger fights, too, fights that were rarer than before but still awful. By that time, we'd learned not to yell most of the time, but it wasn't a total solution.

Even when we were just talking, it felt terrible.

Fortunately, we had more to celebrate than fear. In a mere twenty-four months since becoming parents, we'd learned a lot about relationships. We'd learned how to laugh at ourselves. How to expect the best of each other. How to be nice. How to apologize. We'd learned how to bargain, how to nag the right way. How to talk without yelling. How to talk at all. The question now on my mind: How good was good enough?

How much patience, kindness, maturity, equanimity, selflessness and, well, logic could one reasonably expect from their partner?

Before parenthood took me by the collar and shook me up, I never thought to ask the question. "We treat each other well all the time," I would've told anyone who did. "We don't agree on everything, but we're always nice about it." But, to quote Genevieve, if you graduate parenthood with only one A, you probably got it in Humility. No longer did I assume my marriage was bullet-proof; weaknesses were now frequently recalled. And so, while Year One taught me how to love better, and Year Two, how to communicate my needs, Year Three taught me how to allow better—to accept Matthew as he was, and be at peace.

The argument that best represented our Year Three struggle began, as so many do, with a comment—one that at first seemed innocent enough. After three full months had passed without a mom-and-dad date, we had accepted a party invitation. We dressed up, then got the kids ready, too hurried to admire each other's improved appearance. When we finally arrived at the daycare, we were late and stressed out, and not at all enjoying the experience thus far.

The woman at the front desk didn't seem to notice. She smiled, welcomed Poppy and Harper and introduced them to the other kids. There was a cheerful goodbye, and when we got back in the car, relief came over us.

"It's quiet," I said.

"It's weird, isn't it?" Matthew replied. "They don't cry all that much. But they're really ... loud."

"They're loud in our heads, even when they're not talking or crying."

Matthew laughed. "So true. Hon, I'm glad we're doing this. Thanks for planning it."

"You're welcome. Why don't we do it more often?"

And that's when it happened: Matthew said something I wasn't expecting, something that hurt me more than he could've predicted.

"I don't know. Maybe because we haven't been all that happy lately. We haven't wanted to spend as much time together as we used to."

My first thought: *He doesn't want to spend time with me? Has it really been that bad? Just when I thought things were getting so much better. I really wish he hadn't said that.*

Though I was hurt, I chose not to show it. I changed the subject, not wanting to ruin the night. And once we got to the party, I was glad I'd done so. In the presence of others, we came back to ourselves. We joked and talked, and were on each other's side.

That night, before we went to sleep, I mentioned the comment again, but not in anger, exactly—more like in self-defense. I wanted to tell Matthew why I didn't agree with what he'd said. I wanted to explain to him that after all the ups and downs he may have lost his perspective.

"Honey, what did you mean earlier today when you said we haven't been happy lately?" I asked. "You said you haven't been wanting to spend time with me. Did you mean it?"

"You mean what I said in the car?" Matthew said. "Hon, don't be so sensitive. I didn't mean I don't ever want to hang out. I just meant that things have been rough."

"But it's not all bad, Matthew. We have mostly good days, you know. Don't you appreciate all we've been through and how far we've come?"

"Yes," Matthew said. "But for me, something's still missing. I want to actually feel close to you."

Here, I pulled away from him and sat up in the bed.

"Are you saying that you don't? I feel like you're looking only at what's wrong between us, and ignoring everything else, all the good."

"I know we're not fighting all the time anymore, and I am glad about that. But we're still struggling, you know."

And that was when I started to cry. It was a quiet cry, the kind not easily detected in the dark. To hide it, I merely had to turn my face.

"We had fun tonight," I said after a long, slow breath.

"Yes, we did."

"So that's at least a good sign."

"Yeah. But we need to do better."

"Wow. I had no idea, Hon. I really didn't know you felt this way. You make it sound like I'm a bad wife."

"You're a really good mother, Rachel. But you're not always a good wife. Sometimes, you sort of forget about me."

Matthew put his hand on my back, but I moved away, then let out a loud sob. I left the bedroom, and when Matthew followed, I went to the guest bedroom and shut and locked the door behind me. Then I stayed there the rest of the night.

So he thinks it's all my fault that things aren't perfect between us. Wow. How utterly predictable. I'm the one who planned our date tonight. What has he done lately to reach out? All he does is criticize and assign blame.

Can't he at least see how hard I'm trying? Every day, I'm trying so damn hard. All I want for him is to be happy, and for us to be a happy family. I'm doing the work, and he's just commenting on it.

THE MORNING after the Bad Wife Blowout, I was still upset, and embarrassed, too. I showered in the guest bathroom and skirted around Matt in the kitchen, then carted Poppy away quickly. After our errands, Poppy and I walked to the park. It was cold, but the sun was shining. As I followed her from slide to swing, watching her play, I remembered the advice I'd gotten two years back from Marianne. "Ask yourself what to do. Use your intuition," she'd said. It had worked before. Maybe it would work again.

I started with a review: the fight, my interpretation. My assertion that Matt was blaming me for all of our struggles. I thought about my fear that he didn't feel close to me because he didn't love me anymore. Then I said, "What now?" and got quiet.

The answer came swiftly: "What if none of this matters?"

"What do you mean?" I asked. "Doesn't matter? Of course it does. Matt practically told me he's disappointed with me as a wife. If that doesn't matter, none of it does."

"But did he, Rachel? Is that the real story? And even if it is, what can you do about it?"

"Well, I could talk to him. I could explain to him—calmly, I hope—how hurt and sad the comment made me feel. I could remind him of all the things I've done for him and for our family, how much I do every day. I could ask him to apologize."

"Yes, you could. And it might help. But the way you're feeling, Rachel—this isn't about him, I don't think. Remember the therapist you met at that party who told you that in general, your feelings about a fight are twenty percent about the fight and eighty percent about you? Well, you're in the eighty zone, trying to deal with that part. The twenty is there, but it's just twenty."

"Okay. Say I believe you. What do you want me to do? Nothing? Just let the comment go?"

"Not exactly, Rachel. But what do you think would happen if, just this time, you didn't defend yourself? What if when he got home from work tonight, expecting an argument, you just didn't give it to him?"

"That's crazy. Not defend myself?"

"Think about it."

Then I did. And ... it made sense. It was brilliant. It was brave. *Not defend myself?* I wondered as Poppy and I made our way home. *Is it giving up? Or is it letting go?*

THAT EVENING, when Matthew arrived home, I greeted him cheerfully. I gave him the baby, then started dinner. Over bacon and pancakes, I looked him in the eye, a smile crinkling a corner of mine. "I love you, Honey. I really do. And I'm trying really hard to be a good wife."

"I know that, Rachel. And you are. Of course you are."

I laughed. *Of course I am. Of course I am? Okay.* "Well, that's not how I pictured the end of this fight. No asking for an explanation for my behavior? No hashing it out, figuring it out, dealing with it?"

"Dealing with it? I thought that's what we just did."

"You don't want to know why I got so mad at you?"

"I know why. It was a rough night. You were tired."

I nodded, my smile fading. *I was tired. So it's not that you were insensitive or said mean things. I was tired. That was the problem.* I took a bite of pancake.

So, he doesn't get it. He doesn't know why I was upset. But wait—what's this? Is it ... peace? Am I actually enjoying the feeling of not giving in to my ego, of not proving my point? Maybe. Yes, definitely. I am.

"We should've made vegetables," I said.

"Yeah," said Matthew. "This is ... a lot."

"Tomorrow night, vegetables."

"Vegetables and rice."

My Relationship Journal: December
Lesson: Don't Defend Yourself

BOOK NOTES AND QUOTES:

JOHN GOTTMAN in *Why Marriages Succeed or Fail and How You Can Make Yours Last:*

- There are four main relationship killers: criticism, defensiveness, contempt and stonewalling. Defensiveness causes arguments to escalate and get off track. Keep this bad habit carefully in check.

BYRON KATIE in *Who Would You Be Without Your Story? Dialogues with Byron Katie:*

- "If there is a war in my life, I started it. There's no exception. If the war ends in my life, I end it. I end it, or it doesn't end. No exception."
- Byron Katie also often says, "Defense is the first act of war." The first act of war is not the first mean comment or hurtful behavior. That's just something that happened. War involves a response.

ECKHART TOLLE in *A New Earth: Awakening to Your Life's Purpose:*

- "Nonresistance, nonjudgment, and nonattachment are the three aspects of true freedom and enlightened living."

FATHER THOMAS MERTON in *The Wisdom of the Desert:*

- "And if anyone speak to you about any matter do not argue with him. But if he speaks rightly, say: Yes. If he speaks wrongly say to him: You know what you are saying. But do not argue with him about the things he has said. Thus your mind will be at peace."

MY RELATIONSHIP RESOLUTIONS:

- When confronted, I won't immediately jump to my own defense. Instead, I will say either "interesting thought" or "okay." After listening fully, I might say "I don't

agree," or "I agree." Usually, no elaboration will be required.
- When I do find it necessary to explain my actions and behaviors, I will wait till a time when the other person is willing to listen. Before doing so, I will ask and receive their permission. No exceptions.
- When someone uses an annoyed or angry tone of voice when speaking to me, rather than defend myself, I will ask him if he is feeling okay.
- If someone is hurtful, I will politely ask him to apologize. Doing so doesn't count as defensiveness, just self-respect.
- I will give people—even my partner—the freedom to dislike me at times, and to disagree with me often.

FOR THE FRIDGE:

- "I promise to listen first."
- "I promise to ask permission before telling my side of the story."

11

Appreciate the Gift

One day not long after the Bad Wife Blowout, Matthew did not eat lunch—and it showed. Arriving home after work, he greeted me plaintively. Then he promptly asked for some food.

"I'm hungry," he said, dropping his backpack on the floor and circling around me to the kitchen. "I worked through lunch. What's for dinner?"

"Hi, Hon," I said. I followed him to the kitchen. "I'm not sure. I guess there's not much. I haven't made it to the store."

This time, I wasn't just apologizing to apologize, either; I really did feel bad. Matthew loved food, but cooking wasn't my specialty. I've said many times that I could never cook again and be better off for it.

Mind you, it wasn't always this way. When Matthew and I first got together, I enjoyed making him a well-planned meal. Doing so wasn't a hardship, but one of the little pleasures of my day—a way to express love and be nurturing. After the baby was born, though, food preparation was no longer a productive break from my computer and a chance to do something nice for my partner.

Suddenly, it was just a damned chore.

And so, I slacked off. I cooked less often and less

well, and asked Matthew to order out or cook for himself once in a while. Soon, he was preparing many of his own evening meals, and I was grabbing something quick for the kids and myself before he got home.

"No food?" he asked. "Nothing? Again? Hon, I am really, really hungry."

"I know, Matt. I'm sorry. It was that kind of day."

"It was that kind of day three other times this week."

"Matt, come on. Don't start with me. You can handle making dinner."

"It's not just that. You've been ignoring me. I'm sick of feeling like I'm last place."

"Watch out. You're reading into this. Not cooking doesn't mean I don't love you."

"It feels that way to me."

"Really?"

"Yes."

"I don't know what to do about that, though, Matt. I can't do everything, you know. Something has to fall off my plate. So to speak."

Matthew didn't respond. Instead, he grabbed his car keys and made his way to the front door in the kind of huff that has you defending yourself in your head for the next hour. He left without explanation, then returned with a pile of tacos.

By that time, I was mad, too.

"Was that really so hard?" I asked as I joined him at the dining room table.

"Well, it took forty-five minutes."

I sighed. "Honey, look at me, will you? I'm exhausted. I'm done. I've been going nonstop all day. Every day feels like a marathon. What more do you want me to do?"

"I want food."

I stopped eating my tacos. A hard wind filled my lungs, but I slowly let it out. Then, in that small moment, I made a big decision.

I decided not to be angry.

I took a deep breath, then another one. Then I drank a glass of water. A few tacos in, I managed a smile—a fake smile, but a smile nonetheless.

It helped.

"Do you feel like I don't pay enough attention to you, Matt?"

"Yes," he said, exhaling a bit. "Or maybe, like you don't respect me as much as you used to. Something like that. I don't know."

"I respect you, Hon. I do. I'm doing the best I can."

He didn't respond, and I didn't go on.

That evening, we were quiet—both of us were quiet. Matt genuinely didn't want to talk, and I was practicing my new non-defensiveness strategy. As we sat on the couch together, watching a movie, not touching, I realized something: I was okay.

So, Matt is mad at me, I thought, pretending to pay attention to the screen. *What's the big deal, anyway? I did what I could. I told him I cared about him. I stayed calm and didn't make things worse. He didn't want to hear my side, so here we are, on the couch. Kind of ignoring each other, but we're still together. He'll be mad for a while, but it's okay. It's okay.*

For me, this was a revelation.

That week as Matt slowly regained a more positive perspective on our relationship and I continued to reassure him, I contemplated the lesson a bit further. I asked myself what the point of relationships are, anyway. Are they for making us feel good all the time? No, I realized. That's not what they're for. Relationships—marriages especially—are about growth. They're about learning compromise and communication and hell, just being a nicer person. Would I really want Matt to do everything I wanted him to do as soon as I wanted him to do it? What good would a robot husband be to anyone?

Looking back on that week, I wonder if that was the time that I first knew—truly knew—things were going to be okay with Matt and I. Since having our first child together we'd learned a lot of lessons, but did any of the others affect my attitude toward Matt as completely? In any case, the change that happened inside me that week was real, and it really did take hold. From that time forward, whenever Matt and I disagreed about something significant, I remembered to feel at least a bit grateful for the struggle.

This is how I'm becoming a better person, I told myself. *This is how. Only this. No other way.*

Marriage is a gift, and challenges are part of the package. I see how being married is changing me, and I like it.

THE FOLLOWING WEEK, I saw Genevieve. She asked how things were going with Matt and I. I told her of my change in perspective, of how much I appreciated everything I'd learned over the past several years. And I told her I appreciate myself more than ever, too.

"I really do love everything that's happened with Matthew since becoming a parent," I said. "Not just the good stuff, but the bad stuff, too. It's gotten me from being a wife who truly loves her husband to being a wife who truly loves her husband and also knows how to be good to herself."

"You're stronger," Gen said.

"Yes. I am."

"And motherhood just adds to that."

"Definitely."

"That is what it's about. It's about getting stronger. Not just in marriage–in life. In everything."

"I don't know if I told you this already, but for a while after Poppy was born, I'd get these terrible thoughts about Matt. They'd come to me at night, just overwhelm me. They weren't logical but at the time they felt so frightening. Mostly they were about how hard it was to be married and have kids, but sometimes they were about Matthew specifically. About his character flaws, about how selfish he was. Sometimes, I would just sit and think about all the pain that my kids are going to have to go through in their lives, and how crazy it is to have them knowing this. Well, at some point, it was weird–all those thoughts stopped. Not that I never have a terrible judgment about Matt or bad thoughts about parenting, but I don't get that fear anymore. I don't know how, exactly, but something changed in my head. I have this confidence that basically, we're ... normal. Matt is a normal guy. Our relationship is normal. Our problems are actually pretty insignificant. And when the hard times come, well, like I said, the hard times are just a part of it. They're all just part of the adventure."

Gen nodded. "I haven't gone through that. Not exactly the way you're saying. But I do have a lot of fears for my kids. And I like that attitude you're talking about. In parenting, too, part of what we're teaching our kids is to look at hardship as a good thing. It's real, and it's good, and it's part of what we're doing here. It helps us to grow and get better. Then, hopefully, the bad feelings go away for a while, and when they do we don't have to be afraid of them coming back. They will come back, always. That is their job. And it's okay that they do. Like you said: It's normal."

"It's more than normal. It is a gift."

HOW DID Matthew and I survive those critical first years after Poppy was born? How did we regain the joy in each other we once felt, without significant damage or simmering resentment to show for our experience? Partly it was because we finally stopped the control battles, the tug of war—and when the game did restart, it was usually pretty friendly, and pretty short. First, I learned to short-circuit all my unspoken fears by changing my story about Matt and reminding myself that he loved me. After that, I learned how to talk–how to laugh, even–instead of arguing, and how to let the little stuff go. I was nice, even when Matt didn't seem to deserve it. I found a way to bargain for what I needed. I humbled myself and apologized every chance I got. I finally figured out what Matt needed, biologically-speaking. Then I stopped the nagging and the obsessive self-defense. Finally, when all else failed, I simply embraced the challenge. I reminded myself that marriage is a gift, not in spite of the hard times but because of them, and I remembered how far I had come.

For five years—five wonderful years—after Matthew and I met, our love for each other was easy. We were best friends. We hardly ever fought. Our relationship was straightforward, unmarred. Then we had a baby, and during the three years that followed that event, things were ... well, they were different. Not awful, most of the time. Just challenging. Stretching. The big fights were big, and the little ones were frequent. By the end of those years, though, Matt and I had several key advantages we didn't have before that to us, made the experience well worth the trouble. First, we had a deep understanding of what it takes to be a happy family.

Second, we had a happy family.

And that's what we still have: a family. A happy one. It's been five years since Harper was born, and things have never been better between us. I still talk to Gen and Marianne about my issues with Matt, read the occasional marriage book—even get advice from my inner self once in a while. But most of my self-improvement energy is now focused on parenting my two children. While relationship challenges with Matthew still arise—and with some regularity—the themes of my solutions are often repeated, revisited. I circle back to much of what I learned during that time, and mostly that's enough to get me through. Part of the reason for this is that these themes are fairly flexible. And the other part of the reason is Matthew.

These days, Matthew just gets it in a way he didn't before. Truly, he is a better husband. He talks to me more. He's vulnerable, honest. He is, once again, the best friend I found when we first started dating.

And in some ways, he's even better. He's a dad now, of course, and an excellent one: patient, and giving, and wise. He's not as moody as he used to be—he's learned how to communicate his needs and feelings with more self-awareness. And he's a great deal more helpful. Every single night, his schedule is the family's schedule. He does the laundry. He reads to the kids, brushes their teeth, takes them grocery shopping. And he's in for the hard stuff, too: sleepless nights, discipline, potty training. More important than any single thing he does, though, is the way he makes me feel when he's with me.

These days, every day, I feel loved.

AFTER THE CLASSIC FOOD FIGHT, there was a break in the tension between Matthew and I. Then, for several weeks straight, for a reason unknown to me, Matthew was in a terrible mood. When we went to Home Depot, and I misunderstood what he was looking for, he embarrassed me by speaking rudely to me in the aisle. When to keep his drill away from Poppy I hid it, then couldn't find it again right away, he made a sarcastic comment. Finally, when the car insurance expired before I paid the bill, he chastised me unfairly.

Each time one of these episodes occurred, my first instinct was to defend myself. But I chose to remember my resolution, and find a better way to handle the situation.

A week later, Matthew's mood still hadn't passed, so I decided to practice a few of my other newfound skills. At dinner one evening, I smiled across the table, then pointed out something Matthew did that I appreciated. "You did the dishes yet again, I noticed," I said. "Thanks, Hon. That's a really big help."

Matthew smiled back, and seemed to feel calmer.

"You're welcome," he said. "Thanks for noticing, Rachel."

Then I went in for the kill.

"Hon, I know you've been frustrated with me lately. It seems like something is really bothering you. Do you want to talk about it? Are you okay?"

"Yeah, I guess there is something," he said. "I mean, I'm fine, mostly. But work has been totally sucking, and I hate it. Sometimes I wish I could just quit and move on. Do real estate, like I've always wanted. But this is a good job and I don't know how I'd match the pay. So, here we are. You know."

"Well, let's talk about it. Let's try to figure something out. But can I make a small request?"

"Of course."

"When you're feeling this way—and I know this is hard—can you just not take it out on me? Don't get mad at me for little things that don't matter. Talk to me about the real problem instead."

Matt frowned. "Yeah, I can do that," he said. And with that, the matter was resolved.

My Relationship Journal: December
Lesson: Appreciate the Gift

BOOK NOTES AND QUOTES:

SUE JOHNSON in *Hold Me Tight: Seven Conversations for a Lifetime of Love*:

- The bond of couplehood is similar to the bond between mother and child. It is a primary attachment that provides us with a large portion of our needed security, communication and love.

MATT KAHN in *Whatever Arises, Love That: A Love Revolution That Begins with You*:

- When so-called bad stuff happens, don't fight, don't negotiate—just sit with the pain for a while. When the time is right, you'll know how to handle the problem, but until then, allow yourself to feel what you feel.
- When a feeling is "honored and given permission to be," it eventually dissolves

of its own accord—no striving, no fighting, no negotiation needed.
- Your negative experiences can actually become your greatest gifts, "the source of your own fulfillment."
- No matter how many problems you successfully fix, life will always bring you more. So if you want peace in your life, learn to love what arises.

PEMA CHODRON in *When Things Fall Apart: Heart Advice for Difficult Times*:

- "To stay with that shakiness—to stay with a broken heart, with a rumbling stomach, with the feeling of hopelessness and wanting to get revenge—that is the path of true awakening."
- "Those events and people in our lives who trigger our unresolved issues could be regarded as good news ... We don't need to try to create situations in which we reach our limit. They occur all by themselves, with clockwork regularity."

MY RELATIONSHIP RESOLUTIONS:

- I will be grateful for the challenges marriage brings. If Matthew was perfect, how would I grow? Marriage is one of the most complex, intense relationships in life—and the best opportunity I have to learn to love unconditionally.
- When painful stuff happens, like an argument with Matthew, I won't try to fix it right away. Instead, I'll find a quiet place, and just sit with the feeling. Only

when I'm ready to move on will I do so, even if it takes several hours or days.
- I will remember that Matthew doesn't have to be perfect for me to be happy. I'm tough; I can handle a few flaws.

FOR THE FRIDGE:

- "I promise to remember that one of the best parts of marriage is how it helps me grow."

Appendix One
THE CHEAT SHEET

One morning, you wake up to a note on the fridge reminding your partner to treat you better. You probably don't mind seeing that, do you? Here, then, a cheat sheet with all of the main lessons in this book. My advice: post it flagrantly. It's just a nice thing to do.

LESSON: CHANGE YOUR STORY
For the Fridge:

- "I promise to believe your intentions are good."
- "I promise to double-check my story about you."

LESSON: DON'T FIGHT. JUST TALK INSTEAD.
For the Fridge:

- "I promise not to discuss an issue unless it's worth the tension it will cause and unless I've given it some time."

LESSON: DON'T MAKE IT INTO A BIG DEAL
For the Fridge:

- "I promise to under react."

LESSON: BE UNCOMFORTABLY NICE
For the Fridge:

- "I promise to use a kind, respectful tone of voice, even when upset."

LESSON: SHAMELESSLY BARGAIN. (AND ALWAYS HAVE A BOTTOM LINE.)
For the Fridge:

- "I promise to negotiate, not nag."
- "I promise to focus mainly on solutions, not emotions."

LESSON: APOLOGIZE EVERY CHANCE YOU GET
For the Fridge:

- "I promise to take every opportunity to say I'm sorry."

LESSON: CHANGE YOUR PARTNER THE RIGHT WAY
For the Fridge:

- "I promise not to nag you to change, but to gently encourage it instead."
- "I promise to mirror back to you the change I want to see."

LESSON: BRUSH UP ON YOUR ENDOCRINOLOGY
For the Fridge:

- "I promise to focus on solutions, not emotions."
- "I promise to understand that your needs are real."

LESSON: DON'T DEFEND YOURSELF
For the Fridge:

- "I promise to listen first."
- "I promise to ask permission before telling my side of the story."

LESSON: APPRECIATE THE GIFT
For the Fridge:

- "I promise to remind myself that one of the best parts of marriage is how it helps me grow."

Appendix Two
REPLACEMENT STATEMENTS

We human-types repeat ourselves a lot. Throughout the day we rely on a handy set of go-to statements in order to preserve precious brain power.

"Go slow," we tell our toddlers. "Use your words. Be patient. Take turns."

"It's for the best," we say to our friends. "It'll all work out."

We say these things many, many times.

My husband hears a lot of the same stuff from me, too: "Can you wash the dishes?" "Don't stay up too late" and "Take the baby" are at the top of my list.

A bad mantra can be a hard habit to break.

Fortunately, a good mantra can be a hard habit to break, too. My advice: Pay extra attention to your oft-repeated statements, evaluating how well they help you achieve your goals. Then consider replacing a few of them with a nicer, more effective version.

Here are a few feel-good statements that can replace a whole variety of feel-bad ones.

Instead of "I can't believe you did/said that" or "You are such a jerk," try:

- "Are you feeling grumpy today, Honey?"
- "Are you feeling unloved today?"
- "Are you okay today? Is anything wrong?"
- "Is there anything I can do?"
- "Do you want to talk about it or would you rather wait?"
- "Hey! That wasn't nice."
- "I love you. I know you mean well. But I don't understand the reason you did this. Can you explain, please?"

Instead of a sarcastic "you're welcome," try:

- "Will you say *thank you*, please?"

Instead of "It's not my fault," or "You're the one who ...," try:

- "I'm sorry."
- "That wasn't nice of me."
- "I'm feeling grumpy today."
- "Do you want to know why I did that?"
- "Do you want me to explain now or would you rather wait till later?"

Instead of "I am so mad at you," try:

- "I am feeling angry right now, but it will pass."
- "Watch out. I might have to squish you/tickle you/[insert other completely comical threat]."

Instead of "You aren't listening to me," try:

- "Do you want me to explain more, or do you want me to just listen to your thoughts and we can talk about my side later?"

Instead of "No, I'm not going to do that for you," try:

- "I'm not going to do that right now. But I love you."

Instead of "Stop ignoring me," try:

- "I am feeling lonely today."
- "I am feeling neglected today."
- "I am feeling unappreciated today. Will you do something nice for me?"
- "Do you appreciate me?"
- "Do you love me?"
- "Do you want to cuddle?"

Instead of "Well, 'night, Hon," try:

- "I love you. I really, really love you. Good night."
- "I want you to know I respect you. Good night."
- "I'm truly glad you're my partner, Hon. Good night."

Appendix Three
STORIES FROM THE FIELD

Fights are like trees: each one is different, and yet, there are some basic shared traits. Investigating the details of a particular tree—or a particular argument—can help us notice truths that apply more generally. Here, in interview format, are several specific, true accounts of fights couples have had (and mostly, but not always, successfully resolved). Some of the interviewee names have been changed.

GISELLE
"I WANT TO SCREAM: 'IT'S FIXABLE!'"

Giselle is a forty-year-old mother of two. She has been married for seventeen years.

Mollie: Can you remember a time when your marriage felt extremely difficult? What was the problem and how did it begin?

GISELLE: I remember it like it was yesterday. It was when our second kid was born. At that time, we were both very successful in our careers and lived in a beautiful new home, with nice cars and basically all you could ask for. The problem for us was that we didn't really respect each other. We hadn't learned how to have a productive disagreement and talk through things. Being two very stubborn individuals, we thought we could change each other into the molds we wanted by not backing down in a fight. Ever.

The second child's birth really brought this all to light. Having all we could ask for just wasn't enough anymore. We decided that we were either going to live separate lives or work for it and that's when we reached out for help. Honestly, at that time, while he wanted us to survive, I thought we didn't have a chance and was prepared to move on. I just couldn't take that step, though, partly due to my faith.

So, we tried a year's worth of counseling. It helped. But, what really helped was just maturity and learning that we fell in love for a reason and it all can be fixed as long as we're both willing to at least try. Now, we know that fighting is just a big waste of time and actually listening to each other is way more effective, no matter the outcome.

If I'd only known then what I know now. When couples think they're doomed, I want to scream "It's fixable!" and "I was there."

MOLLIE: **What was one specific argument that you had that showed the lack of respect and ability to communicate?**

GISELLE: To be totally transparent, what sticks out in my head at the moment is when I called him to tell him I was pregnant with baby number two and his response was, "What the fuck!" That wasn't fun.

MOLLIE. **Tell me more about that.**

GISELLE: Okay. Let me set the stage. We were living in my husband's hometown at the time and had been for about seven years. By then, we had made good friends, but they were more like the kind of friends that were fun to party with and we never really opened up to them for help and support with our marriage (or with any intimate feelings for that matter). It's a habit for both of us to not be vulnerable anyway.

When I told my husband about being pregnant with baby number two and he responded badly, I just retreated further and never really talked about my feelings to him or anyone else. Instead, we fought a lot about other stupid things and never really dealt with our real feelings. I was really hurt at the time and felt alone but never said that to anyone. At this point, we were so distant from each other we basically were just co-existing.

When the new baby was a year and a half old we moved back to my hometown to be closer to my family. At that time, I thought either we'd get divorced and it'd be better for me to have my family around, or we'd work it out and it'd still be better to shake things up and have a stronger support system. We started counseling there, too.

It took a while, and things still aren't perfect but definitely worth the move and surrounding ourselves with supportive people. We communicate much better now and know how, when in an argument, to listen to each other more and to do our best to at least hear what the other person is saying.

Since then (the past eight years or so) I'm so grateful we didn't give up on us. We both love our kids and learned so much along the way. We actually like each other and love each other now.

CAL
"FINALLY, OUR HOUSE FEELS LIKE A HOME"

Cal, age forty-four, has four children with his wife of twenty years.

Mollie: Is there an argument that just keeps coming up between you and your wife?

CAL: Many of the long-running arguments that we have seen to be centered around the lack of defined roles in our relationship. We are both products of the feminist movement—women aren't going to be forced to be at home taking care of children and cooking dinner! So the systems of our household are perpetually left leaderless as both adults strive for success and validation outside our home.

This lack of definition has plagued us since the days we just started living together and couldn't agree on who did what chores and who was responsible for what. It's rather embarrassing to say that we still run across these problems twenty years later. At least a few generations ago they had one person who gathered resources and one person who saw that those resources were well managed in producing a family. Now we are both responsible for everything, and that leads to chaos and frustration for us.

MOLLIE: **Can you give me more specifics? Which chores are still up for grabs? Which chores have you come to an agreement on?**

CAL: We have written out three sheets of information for the family. One sheet gives our vision, values, expectations and measures of success. It's funny that after being married over twenty years we are still working out what our vision for our home is. We've had other vision statements in the past, but they seem to have a finite life span. The vision needs to be renewed and revived periodically; for us, it seems like we can agree on one for about two years.

The next sheet shows the systems we are working on to make the household run more smoothly. We started with agreeing on twenty minutes of cleaning and that's going really well thus far (maybe for the past two months). We're still working on figuring out the rest.

Finally, we have a chores sheet. This is laminated (yes, we have a laminator and every family needs one!). We assign and check off the chores using a dry erase marker. There are six of us, and six people cleaning a single area isn't going to work, so we have two or three areas separated out into five days (our goal is to clean five days per week). We schedule the cleaning via group text message at least two hours ahead of time. Then we assemble at the table, pick a day, assign the jobs, start the timer, start some music, and clean for twenty minutes. If someone finishes early, they get re-assigned to another job until we have all worked for twenty minutes. We clean with whoever is home at the time, even if it's only a couple of us.

This cleaning system has finally gotten our house to feel like a home. We all now have clean, paired socks and vacuumed hallways.

Bedroom cleaning is handled by a different system of weekly room inspections.

MOLLIE: **Any other ongoing arguments?**

CAL: Nothing is jumping to mind. My wife and I are pretty low-key people, but we have still managed to have some pretty turbulent times in our marriage. This point isn't one of them. Our kids are now 18, 16, 14 and 11. They are old enough that they are becoming self-sufficient, but young enough not to realize how clueless they are in the real world. It's a frustrating time. I think we've been handling it well, overall, but have been far from perfect.

MOLLIE: **Finally, how much do you enjoy your marriage? Is it worth the hardship?**

CAL: I do enjoy my marriage. The sex is amazing, and that's a large part of male happiness. Consistent access to a female is success in an evolutionary sense. Beyond just meeting physical needs, my wife is a wonderful friend who I still enjoy having dinner with or accompanying to one of our children's events. I made a really good decision before we started dating: I had just had a mediocre dating experience with a pretty red-haired girl, who treated me like a distraction. Based on that experience, I decided that the next person I was going to spend my time with would be one who I enjoyed being with. My wife is remarkable in that I was always sorry when the evening came to an end; there never seemed to be enough time.

Twenty-three years later, I still think that was a wise decision. I haven't had the most exciting life from the outside, but I've enjoyed most minutes because I made a really good choice. I married an honest friend who I really enjoyed being around. Fights come and go, but we still like having dinner, watching a movie or doing a project together. Even when we are at our worst, there has always been that underlying layer of friendship and enjoyment that we fell back on. It's a pretty amazing connection.

ZURIE

ZURIE: "We Have Two Big Rules in Our House"

ZURIE IS 40 years old and has been with her partner for eight years.

MOLLIE: What have some of your biggest disagreements as couple been about?

ZURIE: We don't have children, just cats, which might be why our biggest fight so far was about cats (except not really). Before that, our biggest struggle was learning to grocery shop together without murderous thoughts.

MOLLIE: Tell me more about that.

. . .

ZURIE: It was a thing when we first moved in together. He works from home and I was working in an office. We both dislike the task, so we do it together (unless circumstances prevent it.)

I made a comment a while back about two types of people (on a spectrum): basically, planners and non-planners. My husband is squarely a planner. Lists, schedules, plan of attack. I can (and do) plan, but can also can make a quick decision just to get something done.

So basically, we had several things going wrong.

- I'm an introvert and being at the office all day exhausts me. He works from home, so he's excited to go out.
- We weren't functioning off a list, so we were buying random things that we did/didn't need and still having to figure out dinners after.
- We both wanted to shop how we were used to shopping.

I got mad at him for staring at stacks of American cheese for entirely too long trying to determine the best price on something that I felt didn't matter. He challenged me when I just grabbed a gallon of milk. "Why *that* milk? Do you like it better? This one's cheaper."

After several months and lots of sit-downs and me being mad, then him being frustrated (not huge fights but intense talks), we've figured out and refined our system:

- I frequently save recipes that I think we'll enjoy that are healthy enough for me and easy enough for him. We pick two for the week and build a list off of that.

- We grocery shop on Sundays so I'm not tired and we have a date night once a weekish so he gets out of the house. He has also finally, just this summer, gotten a laptop to give himself the ability to leave the house once in a while.
- There are brands I'm loyal to. When it's time to pick up those, I tell him to kick rocks off to the toilet paper aisle to find us the best deal. I give in to him on the generic canned beans because I don't care and he lets me buy the expensive canned tomatoes without argument.

It works so much better now. We usually have as good a time as you can at the grocery store. And I even stay quiet when he asks the clerk to put the milk in bags (which is silly because the gallons have handles!).

MOLLIE: You seem like a pretty good problem solver. Do you use these same negotiating skills in other areas of your relationship?

ZURIE: We don't have to formally negotiate too often. We try and function as a team so if one person is doing something, the other dives in to help. We've got two big rules in our house:

- Everyone gets what they need.
- You have to ask for what you need.

Spats are usually due to me not being able to sort out what I'm feeling before I get crabby.

MOLLIE: I love those rules! The needs of one person can be dramatically different from the needs of another. Beautiful way to phrase this concept.

So what was the cat thing about?

ZURIE: We fought about when to get a new cat after our last two girls died in the spring. I wanted to get a new one and he wasn't ready.

Honestly, it was 100 percent me not slowing down to figure out what I was feeling so I could verbalize it. Eventually I just realized that I was in an enormous amount of pain and just wanted something to help. I was deeply disappointed that he wasn't ready even though it was valid.

Once I worked through all that emotion, I was able to explain what was going on. I apologized and he listened and we compromised. We got new kitties sooner than he was ready for and later than I wanted, but they're perfect.

MOLLIE: Is there something about your partner you have tried to change? What was your strategy? How well did it work?

ZURIE: Sure, there are things we've tried to change about each other. He's organized, but holy cow was his apartment filthy when he moved out. I'm clean, but completely disorganized. Before we moved in together, we talked a lot about chores and values. He sees the value in having things clean, though he just doesn't notice it. I see the value in having things organized (being able to find my keys is amazing) but I'm not always as good about it as him.

I think we've both really tried to be patient with each other. There are times when I have to remind him that it's okay if I haven't put something back where it belongs because there's a reason I didn't or whatever. And I have 100 percent complained to myself after he does the dishes that he didn't scrub down the stove. But I also know that criticizing will just make a person shut down, so I think a lot about "how much does this matter?" I've had to teach him how to clean the bathroom and the floors and the kitchen and the reasons behind it. He really gives it a good-faith effort, so I let go of the fact that he doesn't see the dirt and is always surprised that it's time to clean. It just doesn't matter.

MOLLIE: Can you think of a time you became overly defensive in an argument? Tell me the story.

ZURIE: When we first met, he used to tell a joke, then say, "Get it? It's funny because ..." and I used to feel like he thought I was so stupid or not funny if he felt he had to explain every joke to me. My dad was really hard on my brother and me and would ask us if we were stupid whenever we did something wrong, so he was really stepping on a land mine he didn't know was there. I finally told him one night how much it hurt my feelings. I was angry and asked flat-out if he thought I was an idiot. He was horrified. Apparently, this was just something he had always said as part of a joke. He thought it was funny and had no idea that I took it personally.

While I was relieved that I was misinterpreting, I also made it clear that I was never going to be okay with it. He'd done it for so long that he wasn't sure he could just stop. So we decided that he would make an honest attempt to say it less and I would make an honest attempt to let it roll off my back if he did say it. And honestly, I haven't heard it in years.

MOLLIE: Do you think it's important to apologize even when you weren't exactly in the wrong, or do you save your apologies for the important stuff?

ZURIE: We tend to apologize to each other when we feel it's warranted. Honestly, we don't fight dirty or often so I don't feel that I've had to apologize when I wasn't exactly wrong.

MOLLIE: Generally speaking, how much do you enjoy partnership? What do you like about it?

ZURIE: I love being married. We haven't reached a point yet where I've considered it difficult or a hardship. I really enjoy being on a team with him. I can be exactly who I am at any given moment with him. I can be ridiculous and silly or sad or a big baby and he understands and loves it. I love doing the same for him. I love hearing him sing songs to the cats or laugh at his podcasts while he works. I am so delighted and thankful to be with him and he seems to feel the same way. We married late-ish—I was thirty-seven and he was forty—so we'd gone through those mid-twenties struggles already and had started establishing our own values when we met. Maybe that has something to do with it.

MOLLIE: Do you have any ongoing arguments that can't seem to be resolved, even with your great communication skills?

ZURIE: Not that I can think of, so definitely nothing major. Things are tough right now for us, but not between us. I'm lucky: he's funny, responsible, hard working, compassionate and loyal. We make a good team.

SIMON
"I WAS ALWAYS APOLOGIZING AND BLAMING MYSELF"

Simon is a writer and retiree living in Indiana. He has been divorced twice and is now living with his cat.

Mollie: Can you remember a particularly difficult argument you had with your wife when you were married? What was the problem?

SIMON: Here's one that stands out: my second wife was leaving all her shoes downstairs on the living room floor. I was constantly tripping over them, stepping on them, etc. At the time we were in counseling. The counselor asked me if there was anything my wife could do to help a bit with our problems, and I said that I knew an easy one: she could just pick up her shoes in the living room each night and put them in the bedroom closet. Her response was that she was so tired when she got home from work that she couldn't carry them up there. I said to the counselor that I would fix that. I would move the shoe rack down to the closet next to the door.

As soon as we got home, I did that. Then, after a

few days, I found all her shoes from work laying on the bedroom floor upstairs. Previously, in anger, I had thrown them all upstairs. This time I threw them all downstairs. Childish, but I felt better.

MOLLIE: Why does this particular argument stand out to you?

SIMON: It was such a difficult one because it was after this that I knew she did not want the marriage anymore and was not really trying.

MOLLIE: Looking back, was it really about the shoes? If not, what was it really about?

SIMON: It was about the shoes, but deeper than that, it was about how she wasn't trying at all to help matters even in small ways. This argument was what teetered the marriage into a divorce. It was a horrible experience. I know there were parts that were my fault if for no other reason than not communicating openly, though I really tried.

MOLLIE: If you were still married and the shoes situation happened again, would you respond the same way? If not, how would you handle it differently?

SIMON: No, not at all. My life has changed direction entirely. I would, first, ask my wife to have a conversation. Then I would tell her what has happened and ask why. When we truly figured that out, we would discuss how to approach it and what would be something that works for both sides.

I now fully believe and insist on honest, open communication. I believe in love and know that it is the only true emotion. If we absolutely could not reconcile the situation or the marriage, then an amicable divorce would still be my choice. That is, one still rooted in love between us as human beings and souls if nothing else.

My advice is to treat everyone as perfect and beautiful and loving. It pays off always, if not now, then later.

MOLLIE: How do you feel about apologizing? Are you used to it, or does it feel hard?

SIMON: Growing up, I always apologized for everything. In my marriage, that happened also. I was always apologizing and blaming myself. I saw myself as a failure and lived up to that in many ways, though I was successful in a lot of things such as education, work, and raising my children. This changed after my stroke. My entire personality changed and I did not see the reason I should apologize so often. This would have caused great conflict in my first marriage. It would have felt better in the end, though, I believe.

Now, apologizing is not hard if I feel I have truly done something wrong. I, basically, refuse to apologize for something I didn't do or just to end a fight or an unpleasant conversation.

. . .

MOLLIE: Have you ever noticed yourself getting into the habit of using a negative or dismissive tone of voice with your partner on a regular basis?

SIMON: No, but I was very passive-aggressive in my first marriage. I would make promises and not keep them just to get out of an argument. I would blame myself for so much and decide that I needed to placate her to stop the fighting. I learned very early in life to hate fighting and to blame myself for things. I did not like conflicts and avoided them at almost any cost. That is no longer true and, at times, I may argue for my side when it isn't really necessary. I am working on that. I feel I have rights now and they need to be observed as much as anyone else's.

MOLLIE: Have you ever argued about needing more time alone or needing more time with your partner? Were you able to resolve the situation and if so, how?

SIMON: Yes to both of those. My spouse, generally, gave me time alone; however, it was done by her leaving to study or something and giving me a list of things to be done before she got back. I honestly got to the point that I realized she would get upset even if I tried really hard to get things done, telling me they weren't done well enough, or if I did them more slowly and carefully but didn't get them all done. So, when she left, I would play with the kids and watch TV or a video, then, about half an hour before she got home, I would rush around and do a halfway job of all the things. She still yelled, but I didn't care as I had had a good evening.

MOLLIE: Generally speaking, how much do you enjoy marriage? What do you like about it? Is it worth the hardship?

SIMON: After two marriages and two divorces, being in my sixties, and with the children grown, I have decided I don't really care that much about marriage. I think part of this might be because I lost some of my ability to love with the stroke. It doesn't feel the same now and I enjoy the life I have. I would enjoy having someone in my life, but marriage doesn't feel right. The divorces were too hard and took too much of a toll on my life. I don't want another one.

Since I don't want any more children at my age, living together seems more advisable and desirable. I could do that or live in separate homes and spend a lot of time together at either of them or out. I imagine there are some women who would like that as well. We will see. I can see the hardship being worth it to someone not in my position.

KAY
"KNOWING HOW HIS MIND WORKS SAVES
A LOT OF HURT"

Kay is thirty-nine years old. Married for eleven years, she has one stepson and one biological son.

Mollie: Can you remember a particularly difficult argument you had with your husband? What was the problem?

KAY: There are always little misunderstandings but two arguments stick out as the worst and both were during times of intense stress: having a baby and moving. The problem wasn't so much about what was said as about the almost constant irritability and snapping at each other. Especially after the washing machine overflowed for the second time.

MOLLIE: What happened after the washing machine overflowed for the second time?

. . .

KAY: I can't remember specific words, but my husband flipped and snapped at all of us, then I got mad at him for his reaction. It snowballed into yelling for the rest of the day. I remember saying "I hate you" to him. This caused him to pack his bags and leave, but he came back after a few hours and by then we had cooled down.

MOLLIE: **What made this time so stressful for you?**

KAY: Many factors came into play: lack of sleep, the adjustment period, changes in routine, new responsibilities, and figuring out our new roles. When the stress levels subsided, we found our situation greatly improved: a growing family, living in our dream home. And the hard times were forgotten.

We still have our ups and downs, but as we grow older (and wiser?), there are far more ups than downs. I will always be grateful for sticking things out and fixing what was broken instead of throwing it all away.

MOLLIE: **How do you feel about fighting? Are you comfortable with the discomfort? How important or beneficial do you think fighting is?**

KAY: I am comfortable fighting. Yelling doesn't bother me much except when the kids mind it. My husband is the same.

. . .

MOLLIE: **Do you have ground rules for fighting?**

KAY: No ground rules. Just mutual respect and learning what the other person is okay or not okay with.

MOLLIE: **How do you feel about apologizing? Are you used to it, or does it feel hard?**

KAY: I apologize easily. I need to vent almost as much as my husband. Because of this tendency, we get over our issues quickly and are back to normal ASAP. However, I think it would be better to apologize a little less often because when the big things roll around the apology might mean more, and not be something we hear all the time.

MOLLIE: **I hadn't thought of that. Have you ever noticed yourself blowing something your partner did or didn't do out of proportion? What was the result?**

KAY: When I blow things out of proportion, it happens from lack of understanding. Knowing how his mind works saves a lot of hurt. If I don't understand something I am comfortable asking questions until I get a satisfactory answer. Often I think there is only one explanation, only to find out there is another reasonable one.

. . .

MOLLIE: Have you ever argued about needing more time alone or needing more time with your partner? Were you able to resolve the situation and if so, how?

KAY: I have more than enough alone time now that the kids are older and more independent. So I ask for more time together. But my husband needs computer time and nights out with friends, saying we see enough of each other at home. I argue that home time together is not the same as going out time together. Yet I am a homebody and don't pursue the argument enough. And so it turns out that we only go out together a few times per year.

MOLLIE: Generally speaking, how much do you enjoy marriage? What do you like about it? Is it worth the hardship?

KAY: I love marriage. I don't see a lot of hardship, but I'm naturally positive. When things get bad for us they get very bad. But fortunately there have only been a handful of those times and it never lasts long. The key for me is to ignore the blowups. I understand that my husband needs to vent often and that it has nothing to do with me. I don't have to listen to him or engage with him when he is yelling about traffic conditions or his boss's bad attitude.

ROCHELLE
"A FAIR FIGHT IS BETTER THAN IGNORING PROBLEMS OR ISSUES"

Rochelle is a 59-year-old mother of two grown children. She has been married for sixteen years.

Mollie: First, can you remember a particularly difficult argument you had with your partner?

ROCHELLE: Yes. My husband is overweight and has been taking his blood pressure medications inconsistently. Recently we went to the cardiologist who said his blood pressure is off the charts at 180/100 and that this is very dangerous. The doctor prescribed a third medication to bring the pressure down. I asked if there was anything else we could do. He laughed and said, "Yes, diet and exercise." I asked if there was any specific diet or exercise. He has been seeing my husband for years, so he said, "Most people know what to do," and grinned.

In the past, the doctor has given my husband special diets and exercises. He doesn't do them. I've been lovingly suggesting healthy food and exercise for years, but he doesn't want to eat this way. He wants red meat and potatoes only every night. We are now looking at adding a third prescription, which he may or may not take depending on what he wants to do at the time. And if I look at his history for indications, I assume he won't eat well or exercise long-term.

MOLLIE: So you argued about this? What happened?

ROCHELLE: I told my husband I wanted him to take care of himself and eat well and exercise. I was upset and said it loudly. He came back seething and said he was going to do it his way.

In the past, I've tried to use kindness and sweetness to inspire self care change. This time I let out the full-out bitch. I haven't ever really called on her before and she isn't all that skilled. I'm not sure how this will work long term, but it seemed to work for now. Currently he is eating an anti-inflammatory diet where he finds the recipes and does the shopping and we cook together.

MOLLIE: That is very interesting. I have had the same experience at times. Maybe when the yelling is rare, it holds more weight?

ROCHELLE: Yes. I think it was the strong language (and a thrown shoe) that made him pay attention and consider changing to a different, more life-giving diet. I'm really proud of him for making the change and being consistent.

We have had good cerebral conversations about the whys, the underlying feelings, the impetuses. It seems the chats feel good but do nothing to bring about any change and the rage does. I don't really like this because, like I said, I'm not skilled with rage. Also, I'm not sure how I feel about being positively reinforced for rage, but not kindness and sweetness and clarity.

MOLLIE: **Why does your partner have such a hard time with this issue?**

ROCHELLE: Here's how it looks to me. We are valuing different things. I'm fighting for self-care, partnership. It could be from love (I want a vibrant life for him and us) or fear (is he going to die soon?) or anger (I'm not going to keep trying to take care of someone who won't take care of himself).

It's a little more difficult for me to see the problem from his point of view, but it looks like he's fighting for his version of freedom. The underlying thing seems to be, "Nobody is going to tell me what to do. I'll do it my way."

MOLLIE: **Do you think it's important to apologize even when you weren't exactly in the wrong, or do you save your apologies for the important stuff?**

. . .

ROCHELLE: He apologizes more than I do, but he's wrong more than I am! Okay, kidding. Honestly, I don't apologize often. If I've done something I am truly sorry for, I say I'm sorry and I don't do it again.

I don't like apologizing. If I need to I will, but it's not my go-to.

MOLLIE: **How do you feel about fighting?**

ROCHELLE: My preference is talking and kissing but I don't mind fighting sometimes. My husband hates fighting. He saw his parents do it a lot so he avoids conflict at any cost. It's one of the things we are working on. I say a fair fight is better than ignoring problems or issues. Let's just say it all out, get it in the open, feel whatever is true, then move on and love each other.

MOLLIE: **Can you think of a time you became overly defensive in an argument?**

ROCHELLE: When I feel myself becoming overly defensive, I'm pretty sure I have an unresolved issue from the past. You know, you can feel when it is your stuff, not theirs. Time to journal or meditate or pray. This happens when my husband suggests something about children or family, maybe about mistakes I made. More than anything I want to be a good mother but I'm human and have made mistakes, so I get all bent out of shape, even when he says, "You were such a great mother to them" during the conversation. I know that I love them so much and did many, many things well but there were some things that, if could do them again, I'd do differently.

MOLLIE: I can definitely see why you'd feel defensive about that. Have you ever noticed yourself attacking your partner's character rather than addressing his behavior and using "I" statements?

ROCHELLE: I'm clear about the difference between who he is and a behavior. He is my chosen beloved and sometimes his behaviors piss me off.

MOLLIE: Have you ever noticed yourself getting into the habit of using a negative or dismissive tone of voice with your partner on a regular basis?

ROCHELLE: This was one of my biggest complaints about his behavior. I hated the feeling of negative or dismissive tones from him. There was a time when I mocked him with negative phrases he used or the words he'd use to cut off communication. Now when he does it, he at least can see that he's doing it and usually softens and communicates.

MOLLIE: Have you ever argued about needing more time alone or needing more time with your partner?

. . .

ROCHELLE: Yes. He used to work sixteen-hour days and I wanted more time with him. Recently, though, he has been looking for a job and we are now together 95 percent of the time. I actually like being with him. When he gets a job I hope it isn't as demanding as the last one.

MOLLIE: **Generally speaking, how much do you enjoy marriage?**

ROCHELLE: I love it! It's easier, I have someone to love, someone to help me when I need it. My partner is smart so that makes it fun.

MOLLIE: **Is it worth the hardship?**

ROCHELLE: 100 percent.

PETRA
"WE LITERALLY SAT AT THE TABLE AND NEGOTIATED"

Petra, a college student, has been with her partner for six years. They have one child from her previous relationship.

Mollie: Can you remember a particularly difficult argument you had with your partner? How did it start? What was the problem?

PETRA: I remember two very difficult arguments.

The first started because we were with friends and I wanted to go out dancing. At which point, my partner told me he did not want to go because he didn't like who I became around "these people" and that he didn't like who I had been in general for the last few weeks.

We were drinking and got a ride home. The fight continued the whole way until we got home and it escalated. I said some hurtful things, accusing him of being controlling and disrespectful. He snapped and punched something, breaking one of his fingers.

For that moment the issues were his comments

and restriction of activities, but really we had been struggling for a few months because he went through a major life change and started taking it out on me. Not in any sort of abusive way, but he was very short tempered and reactive. He stopped communicating openly with me, affection was gone, and he was getting impatient with our daughter.

The second very difficult argument was more recent, actually. I have been going through some major self-esteem issues and those are showing by lacking trust in my partner. I guess in my head I don't think I'm a very great person, so I don't believe he would choose me over other things.

He had a family trip he wanted to go on with his parents and he did not invite me. I took it incredibly personally and reacted in ways similar to codependent people. I was hurt that I wasn't invited and hurt because I know his mother did not invite me on purpose. (While she may like me, she does not approve of us being unmarried and does not approve of my lack of religion.) I exploded and tried to control his actions and force him into choosing between me or his mother. We fought for a whole week, but instead of trying to communicate calmly or explain emotions, I just threw accusations and forced him to miss the trip (basically).

MOLLIE: **What happened after that terrible week-long argument? How did you work through it?**

PETRA: My partner has a tendency to apply a "fuck it" attitude when he does not want to make a hard choice. Ultimately I told him there was nothing that could happen to undo the hurt of not being invited, and that because of that it did not matter whether he stayed or went on the trip. My feelings were already hurt so he should make the choice that was what he wanted. He went back and forth about it a lot. I calmed my feelings down and realized this was not about me, that I was acting selfishly.

Eventually he missed out on being able to go because he could not make up his mind, which started another fight because he blamed me for missing it. However, he was able to see that it was his indecision and his reactions to my feelings/actions that ruined his trip. After another day or so, he apologized for blaming me and we had some serious talks about the way I handle my occasional codependent feelings. We both agreed to make some changes and have been doing better since.

MOLLIE: **What changes did you make, specifically?**

PETRA: He is working on being more decisive based on what is best for him or what he may want instead of waiting for my approval. I am not going to project my insecurities from past trauma onto him. Instead, I have been waiting to communicate any negative feelings until after I calm down and journal about them, and I am working on being more accepting of his right to alone time.

We also started using "pause" as a safe word, so if one of us is too heated and the other feels it isn't a good time to talk or make decisions we say "pause" and the other respects it, no matter what.

. . .

MOLLIE: Have you ever been able to resolve a conflict with your partner through simple negotiation? Tell me about it.

PETRA: Yes. My partner comes from a family where some physical punishment or negative reinforcement was accepted, and he never felt abused. I, however, had a very abusive father. I will not tolerate physical violence and as a teacher, I try to focus more on communication/positive reinforcement. Well, the time came where our child lied to us for the first time. I wasn't sure how to handle the punishment part of the situation, but he wanted to spank and follow through with a month-long grounding. We literally sat at our table and negotiated what her punishment would be. He suggested the above-mentioned, I vetoed and countered with one week grounding—no spanking. He came back with two weeks grounding and extra chores for a month. We went back and forth until we agreed on repercussions for our daughter lying. We even shook hands and said "deal" at the end.

MOLLIE: Generally speaking, how much do you enjoy partnership? What do you like about it? Is it worth the hardship?

PETRA: I enjoy my partnership very much. I came from a very dysfunctional and loveless family so for me, I have had to learn how to be happy without chaos. I love my partnership because we truly are best friends, we actively *choose* each other daily, and we work together for the best life and happiness possible. For every hardship we have experienced, it is still more than worth it. This love and family is the best thing in the whole world.

MARGARET
"LIFE HAS ITS UPS AND DOWNS, WHATEVER YOUR MATRIMONIAL STATE"

Margaret Bendet is the author of Learning to Eat Along the Way: A Memoir, *the story of a reporter who goes out to interview an Indian holy man and never comes back. It is available at margaretbendet.com. In the book, Margaret writes about leaving her husband in 1975 as part of her journey of self-exploration. She never remarried.*

Mollie: With the benefit of hindsight, what do you see as the fundamental problem in the relationship that made it unworkable?

MARGARET: There's a story in my book that speaks to this.

I'm at home in the afternoon (I worked for an evening newspaper, so I got off work early), and I'm trying to meditate. I'd been introduced to meditation in a hatha yoga class, and I wanted to try to work with it. So, I'm sitting in my project room, watching my breath come in and out, listening to the wind play through the trees in the front yard, and I suddenly hear this voice inside me saying, "Get out of my house!"

I didn't leave the house, but I did leave the room. I went to the kitchen and started getting dinner together and thought a bit about what could possibly be happening. My husband and I had bought this house from the children of the couple who had built it as a retirement home and had then died in it—cirst he, then she, shortly before we bought it.

When my husband came home that night, I said, "You're not going to believe what happened today," and proceeded to tell him my story. He didn't believe it. At all. Any part of it. And he was absolutely furious with me that I even considered that such a thing could happen, that a woman who had been dead for seven years could speak to me. No way! It was all in my mind!

I was flattened by him. He was a lawyer, after all, trained in argument. I had learned this before. There had been times before when he asked me a question, and I knew that no matter I said, I was going to be wrong. In the wrong.

But it didn't matter to me this time because I knew that I was right. I knew this had happened. I had heard this in my mind, but this didn't mean that my mind had created it. My mind had no reason to create it. I hadn't been thinking about this woman. I hadn't been looking for someone to interrupt my attempts at meditation.

At that point, I started looking for answers. It was like, with that experience, some seismic shift had happened in my life. I was introduced to a subtle world that doesn't follow material rules. And with that argument, there was a seismic shift in the marriage as well. This question—which was fascinating to me— verboten in my marriage. So, my husband became someone I couldn't talk with, someone I couldn't share with—someone who wasn't interested in the same questions that interested me.

Any of the other conflicts we'd ever had before this were about how one of us, usually me, didn't measure up to the standards that we both had for our life together. But with this argument, it was clear that we were no longer on the same page. Looking back, I can see that there was no longer anything to work out. I had to either pretend to myself that I hadn't had an experience that was compelling for me, or I had to keep walking in a direction that would, inevitably, take me out of the relationship.

MOLLIE: Was that when you started researching and reporting on metaphysical phenomena? How did doing so change you?

MARGARET: It isn't that I began researching and reporting on metaphysical reality right away, but I did start paying attention to parts of life that can't be measured or proven. It's what's most important. What do I mean by that? Just think about it for a moment. How would you measure love? How would you prove intuition or creativity? How do you quantify the benefits of a quiet mind? You can't. Yet this is what matters most.

MOLLIE: Can you tell me about a conflict you experienced after the divorce? What was the problem?

. . .

MARGARET: Again, in my book there is a chapter about the back-and-forth that happened in our marriage. Initially I entitled the chapter "So, He Grades Your Cooking," and it was about a conversation I'd had with a co-worker when I shared a recipe with her—a recipe that had a little "B+" written in the upper right corner.

When my ex-husband read the manuscript, he was furious about this title and about my description of the argument in the book. He emailed me and pointed out that we graded each other's cooking, that we had cooked together a lot in the beginning, and that the grade was just to show whether or not we wanted to make a particular dish again.

I felt gut-punched by his reaction, but then I thought about it. I responded that he was right—we did cook together—but that this was mainly in the beginning. After a few years, I did almost all of the cooking, and I did end up feeling graded—judged—by his evaluations. But I also told him that if he felt strongly about it, I didn't have to use that story.

The other thing he said, which was more compelling, was to point out to me that I had in my description of our marriage sort of soft-pedaled my own failings. I would go along with things for a while and then I would have blow-ups—eruptions.

"Do you think you were easy to live with?" he asked me. "'The way this reads now, you were just some innocent, looking for the light."

I laughed. I had to. He was absolutely right. My anger was a huge factor in our marriage—in my life—and I truly needed to discuss this in the book.

MOLLIE: What is it like being unmarried? Is it easier?

. . .

MARGARET: In the last forty-five years, I've had many different experiences of being unmarried—just like I had many different experiences of being married in the seven years that I was. Life has its ups and downs, whatever your matrimonial state. I look at the question of whether or not a person should be married in terms of personal growth. In other words, what are the lessons this person needs to learn? If you need to learn about compromise and taking responsibility for more than just yourself, then marriage is an excellent way to do that. If, on the other hand, you need to learn independence and how to care for yourself, then being single is a great way to get those lessons. I have to say that being single has been good for me.

SAMANTHA
"WE HAVE A LOT OF COMMUNICATION RULES"

Samantha has been with her partner for seven years and has one child.

Mollie: Have you ever argued about needing more time alone or needing more time with your partner? Were you able to resolve the situation and if so, how?

SAMANTHA: This is a huge argument with us. I tend to need more together time and he needs more alone time. Sometimes the roles flip, but that's usually our dynamic. The solutions have been revised over the years, but here's where we've ended up: The first thing we had to do was define what alone time and quality time meant. Quality time for me doesn't include family time, double dates with friends, etc. It's time spent talking, doing an activity, or whatever as long as I feel like we're more just zeroed in on each other. Alone time for my partner means complete isolation with no interruptions where he feels like he's 100% off. Then we talked about how much quality time/alone time we needed to feel charged. I only need one night a week of quality time, but he needs at least two nights for his alone time. Then it was about trying to fit that time into an already jam-packed schedule (school, work, social activities and family time already takes up so much of our time).

I will say that the hard thing about the quality time versus alone time thing is that it quickly cycles into a bad pattern: He needs alone time so he secludes himself. I need quality time so I push him to spend time together. He isn't really feeling it, so our time together is half-hearted, then he secludes himself again. I feel hurt because he wasn't as engaged as I wanted him to be, so I push him to hang out again. Rinse and repeat.

MOLLIE: Can you remember a particularly difficult argument you had with your spouse? How did it start? What was the problem?

SAMANTHA: Like I said, our more difficult fights tend to be over how we split time so that everything is fair. I work part-time and go to school full-time. He works full-time and goes to school part-time. Our time is super limited, and it only works if we carefully coordinate our schedules.

When our son was first born, I actually had a full blown identity crisis, which put me into a significant depression. I ended up taking a mental health break from school and became a full-time stay-at-home mom and house runner. All of this was a major adjustment and there were a lot of obstacles in that first year because my depression made it hard for me to feel motivated to do housework. We had a lot of fights back then because he thought I was selfish and unempathetic because I was leaving a bunch of the workload on him, and I thought he was callous for not understanding my mental state. When I decided to go back to school and work, we had to readjust again.

Our work schedules were set, so that part was easy. Housework was fairly easy to divide up, too. Figuring out fair parenting expectations, though, were hard. For one, I was used to being "on" almost all the time. I had a hard time asking for help and I micromanaged him a lot when he was parenting. Our son had to adjust because he was used to defaulting to me for everything. My partner felt like he wanted to be an active parent, and he is more involved than most other dads I know, but he also wanted significant chunks of time carved out for his alone time and he felt entitled to that because he worked longer hours. I would get frustrated because he'd come home from work and turn off habitually. I got resentful because I would balance studying for my midterms and being a mom, while he was more comfortable announcing that he needed uninterrupted study time for his own exams. To be fair, if I told him I needed the time, he would have cooperated. But it was additional emotional labor and having to ask made me feel unsupported.

MOLLIE: "EMOTIONAL LABOR." Yeah, I get that. How do you feel about apologizing? Are you used to it, or does it feel hard?

SAMANTHA: Apologies feel vulnerable and when someone I love is angry with me, it's hard for me to feel openly vulnerable in front of them. So it's hard to apologize sometimes because I feel like I'm acknowledging some things about myself that I might struggle with in a situation where I've caused some kind of pain. I've gotten more comfortable with it over the years, though, and my level of comfort depends on the severity of the situation. When it feels hard, I have to take a few minutes to myself and sit with that uncomfortable feeling before I'm able to own it in front of the other person.

MOLLIE: Do you have ground rules for fighting?

SAMANTHA: We absolutely have ground rules. We call them boundaries, and I think they're an intrinsic part of a healthy relationship. I don't like being yelled at or cussed at. Those things don't have a place in our fights. If we get too heated, we walk away and try again later. My partner requires that our arguments be solution-oriented, so we have a rule that you need to have a solution in mind before you bring up an issue. Even if that's not the solution that ends up being the best fit, it at least it directs the conversation in a more productive way. I'm still practicing that one. Sometimes I need to just talk about my feelings without needing to solve things so in that case I make it a point to preface the conversation with "This is a feelings conversation, not a solution conversation, so just let me get it out".

MOLLIE: What other communication guidelines are helpful for you?

. . .

SAMANTHA: We have a lot of communication rules that basically exist to make sure that we feel like our boundaries are being equally respected. For example, my partner doesn't like it when I throw a bunch of tasks at him throughout the day so I have a running sticky note on my computer for things to talk about or things that need to be done. We discuss it all in one sitting that's convenient.

MOLLIE: Have you ever noticed yourself getting into the habit of using a negative or dismissive tone of voice with your partner on a regular basis? Were you able to resolve that problem, and if so, how?

SAMANTHA: So this one is a dangerous one in my eyes. I don't think anything kills a relationship quite like contempt. I wasn't the one in the habit of using a negative or dismissive tone, but I was on the receiving end of it. I talked openly about the mental health issues in my relationship, and one of the big issues early on was the resentment my partner had for me. I resented him too, but not quite to the same level. We slipped into a bad place where he was using a very negative tone with me frequently. When I recognized how patterned the behavior had become, I basically told him that our relationship isn't going to survive if this continues to be our norm. I told him I couldn't be with someone who thought so little of me, and I couldn't demonstrate that as a normal dynamic for our son. Things didn't change overnight after that talk, but gradually and consistently they improved.

. . .

MOLLIE: Wow! That is a huge win. Generally speaking, how much do you enjoy partnership? What do you like about it? Is it worth the hardship?

SAMANTHA: I am community- and relationship-oriented. I love people. I love building on my relationships with family and friends. And that carries over to my relationship with my partner. I'm just someone who likes to feel connected to people and explore those connections. I think these interpersonal relationships are one of the best things about the human experience.

A long-term relationship with a partner offers a unique experience in that you simultaneously play so many different roles in each other's lives. In the thirteen years that I've known my partner, we have been friends, lovers, housemates, and co-parents. I've learned so much about myself in these different roles. While I've also been given the opportunity to know someone so thoroughly, I've also been utterly understood. We're human, so we're constantly growing and changing, so there's always more to learn about the other person. In my case, it's very much been worth the hardships.

Appendix Four
RECOMMENDED READING

My Favorite Marriage Books:

- *Hold Me Tight: Seven Conversations for a Lifetime of Love,* Dr. Sue Johnson
- *Love Sense: The Revolutionary New Science of Romantic Relationships,* Dr. Sue Johnson
- *Love Is Never Enough: How Couples Can Overcome Misunderstandings, Resolve Conflicts, and Solve Relationship Problems Through Cognitive Therapy,* Aaron T. Beck M.D.
- *The Seven Principles for Making Marriage Work: A Practical Guide from the Country's Foremost Relationship Expert,* John Gottman
- *Eight Dates: Essential Conversations for a Lifetime of Love,* John Gottman, Julie Schwartz Gottman, Doug Abrams and Rachel Carlton Abrams
- *The Relationship Cure: A Five-step Guide to Strengthening Your Marriage, Family, and Friendships,* John Gottman and Joan DeClaire
- *And Baby Makes Three: The Six-Step Plan for Preserving Marital Intimacy and Rekindling*

- *Romance After Baby Arrives*, John Gottman and Julie Schwartz Gottman
- *His Needs, Her Needs: Building an Affair-Proof Marriage*, Willard F. Harley Jr.
- *Venus on Fire, Mars on Ice: Hormonal Balance– The Key to Life, Love and Longevity*, John Gray
- *The Seven Principles for Making Marriage Work: A Practical Guide from the Country's Foremost Relationship Expert*, John Gottman
- *Love Is Never Enough: How Couples Can Overcome Misunderstandings, Resolve Conflicts, and Solve Relationship Problems Through Cognitive Therapy*, Aaron T. Beck M.D.
- *Marry Him: The Case for Settling for Mr. Good Enough*, Lori Gottlieb
- *The Surprising Secrets of Highly Happy Marriages: The Little Things That Make a Big Difference*, Shaunti Feldhahn
- *For Better: How the Surprising Science of Happy Couples Can Help Your Marriage Succeed*, Tara Parker-Pope
- *The Proper Care and Feeding of Husbands*, Dr. Laura Schlessinger
- *The 5 Love Languages: The Secret to Love that Lasts*, Gary Chapman

Spirituality Books with Practical Advice on Relationships:

- *Whatever Arises, Love That: A Love Revolution That Begins with You*, Matt Kahn
- *When Things Fall Apart: Heart Advice for Difficult Times*, Pema Chodron
- *The Wisdom of No Escape: How to Love Yourself and Your World*, Pema Chodron

- *The Power of Now: A Guide to Spiritual Enlightenment*, Eckhart Tolle
- *A New Earth: Awakening to Your Life's Purpose*, Eckhart Tolle
- *The Complete Conversations with God*, Neale Donald Walsch
- *Full Catastrophe Living: Using the Wisdom of your Body and Mind to Face Stress, Pain, and Illness*, Jon Kabat-Zinn
- *The Work of Byron Katie: An Introduction*, Byron Katie
- *Loving What Is: Four Questions That Can Change Your Life*, Byron Katie and Stephen Mitchell
- *I Need Your Love–Is That True?: How to Stop Seeking Love, Approval, and Appreciation and Start Finding Them*, Byron Katie and Michael Katz
- *Who Would You Be Without Your Story?: Dialogues with Byron Katie*, Byron Katie

Good Self-Help and Psychology Books:

- *The Feeling Good Handbook*, David Burns
- *Conquer Your Critical Inner Voice: Counter Negative Thoughts and Live Free from Imagined Limitations*, Robert Firestone
- *The Science of Happiness: How Our Brains Make Us Happy–And What We Can Do to Get Happier*, Stefan Klein
- *The How of the Happiness: A New Approach to Getting the Life You Want*, Sonja Lyubomirsky
- *Switch: How to Change Things When Change Is Hard*, Chip Heath and Dan Heath
- *Predictably Irrational: The Hidden Forces That Shape Our Decisions*, Dan Ariely

- *Happiness: Unlocking the Mysteries of Psychological Wealth,* Ed Diener and Robert Biswas-Diener
- *What Makes Your Brain Happy and Why You Should Do the Opposite,* David DiSalvo
- *Authentic Happiness: Using the New Positive Psychology to Realize Your Potential for Lasting Fulfillment,* Martin Seligman
- *The Happiness Advantage: How a Positive Brain Fuels Success in Work and Life,* Shawn Achor
- *Flourish: A Visionary New Understanding of Happiness and Well-being,* Martin Seligman
- *The Power of Habit: Why We Do What We Do in Life and Business,* Charles Duhigg
- *Molecules of Emotion: Why You Feel the Way You Feel,* Candace Pert
- *Breaking the Habit of Being Yourself: How to Lose Your Mind and Create a New One,* Joe Dispenza
- *Daring Greatly: How the Courage to Be Vulnerable Transforms the Way We Live, Love, Parent, and Lead,* Brene Brown
- *Telling Yourself the Truth: Find Your Way Out of Depression, Anxiety, Fear, Anger, and Other Common Problems by Applying the Principles of Misbelief Therapy,* Marie Chapman and William Backus

Parenting Books that Relate to Marriage, Too:

- *If I Have to Tell You One More Time …: The Revolutionary Program That Gets Your Kids To Listen Without Nagging, Reminding, or Yelling,* Amy McCready

- *Parenting with Love and Logic: Teaching Children Responsibility*, Foster Cline
- *Raising an Emotionally Intelligent Child: The Heart of Parenting*, John Mordechai and Joan Declaire
- *The Child Whisperer, The Ultimate Handbook for Raising Happy, Successful, and Cooperative Children*, Carol Tuttle

A Few Good Marriage Memoirs:

- *How to Stay Married: The Adventures of a Woman Who Learnt to Travel Light in Life, Love and Relationships*, Mary-Lou Stephens
- *Love Warrior: A Memoir*, Glennon Doyle Melton
- *Committed: A Skeptic Makes Peace with Marriage*, Elizabeth Gilbert
- *The Wishing Year: A House, a Man, My Soul: A Memoir of Fulfilled Desire*, Noelle Oxenhandler
- *Surprised by Joy*, C.S. Lewis
- *A Severe Mercy*, Sheldon Vanauken

Dear reader,

We hope you enjoyed reading *Fights You'll Have After Having a Baby*. Please take a moment to leave a review, even if it's a short one. Your opinion is important to us.

Discover more books by Mollie Player at https://www.nextchapter.pub/authors/mollie-player

Want to know when one of our books is free or discounted? Join the newsletter at http://eepurl.com/bqqB3H

Best regards,

Mollie Player and the Next Chapter Team

About the Author

Mental health counselor in training Mollie Player attempts feats of great strength, then writes about what happens. Her goals include: daily meditation, homeschooling her kids, not arguing with her spouse and, of course, finding inner peace. Her plans don't always work out, but when they do, the results are awesome. And when they don't, well, it keeps things interesting.

Get her free ebooks and online serials at mollieplayer.com.

You might also like
What Girls Are Good For by David Blixt:

To read the first chapter for free go to:
https://www.nextchapter.pub/books/what-girls-are-good-for

Fights You'll Have After Having a Baby
ISBN: 978-4-86751-428-3
Mass Market

Published by
Next Chapter
1-60-20 Minami-Otsuka
170-0005 Toshima-Ku, Tokyo
+818035793528

30th June 2021

www.ingramcontent.com/pod-product-compliance
Lightning Source LLC
LaVergne TN
LVHW032010070526
838202LV00059B/6374